MONDAY IS STILL COMING

Life-Changing Reflections
Beyond Sunday

By

Tracy La'Nai Clark

ISBN 9781792749841

Dedicated to the loving memory of

My Parents

Your words left an indelible image upon my life,

Your life, even more.

MOM'S MEMOS

Pages in this book entitled "Mom's Memos" are dedications to my mother's writings. My mom, Brenda Joyce Huntley Clark, loved the Lord and the practical application of the Word. Although, she never professed to be a writer, she would always jot down a few notes on a page and how it applied to a scripture and our lives in Christ. I came across something she wrote and deemed it an appropriate explanation of this section: "The saying is 'A picture is worth a thousand words.' They are the windows of our own speech where the truth shines through, even on a cloudy day. Many, today, are not telling stories in a sermon. I still prefer to hear the simple, scriptural, spiritual teachings and preaching of Jesus Christ. For His teachings were truth, plain and simple."

Inserted within the following pages, you will find "Mom's Memos" in her own words. May this book be a testament to the truth, plain and simple.

FOREWORD

BY: REV. PHYLLIS BYRD OCHILO

Much has been written about the opioid crisis in the United States. Many of these opioid addicts started out using prescribed medicine to relieve pain, not knowing how addictive the drugs were. We attend church Sunday after Sunday; many of us go because we are seeking relief from the pains of life. Sunday morning becomes the "Balm in Gilead" when we hear the choir sing our favorite songs that touch the depths of our being and the pastor/minister preaches a sermon that was written "just for me." Reverend Clark, in her book, states that "the excitement of the Sunday sermon wears off on Monday." Then, the three diseases set in: *defeat, depression,* and *despondence.* These disease(s) have become habitual, familiar, and a comfortable way of being. What happened to "Pastor, you preached to me?" How do we respond to the Word of God which touched us deeply? What is our responsibility? Sunday sermons are not opioids that temporarily relieve the pains of life. They are not quick fixes. Reverend Tracy Clark challenges us to move beyond the excitement of the spirit-moving sermon to a sustainable, transformational faith.

The preached word and the choir that minister to us in song should connect us to God, not a momentary good feeling. They should connect us to a faith which is sustainable and transformational. That sustainable and transformational faith derives from the sermon we've heard, as well as other aspects of the worship service as it connects/points us to God. This deep connection to God causes us to hear from God afresh. This renews our trust in God and deepens our faith and resolve to "examine ourselves" as we face the Monday(s) in our lives. The sermons that we hear, the Bible studies we attend, and the ministry of music in the church open us up to the "chrysalis" process of God.

The chrysalis is this betwixt and in-between stage in the life of a butterfly when they leave the infant stage of life and become an adult. Our Sunday faith opens us up to the chrysalis process of God, which allows Him to transform us, our circumstances, habits, and the three Ds in our lives, which bind us and hold us back. Transformation, like the life cycle of a butterfly, is not a quick fix. The in-betwixt and in-between life cycle of a caterpillar finds itself, one day, hanging upside down on a twig or a roof of a house. The caterpillar is not defeated, depressed, or despondent because of the new stage of life it is being called to. Rather, the caterpillar fortifies and prepares itself for the change. This is caterpillar faith that we need as Christians in order to transform the three Ds that rule our lives to the three Ps: *power, patience, and prayer.* The caterpillar faith knows that it has, within itself, the God-given power to spin a protective cover. The caterpillar faith knows that patience is an important part of the process because, even though it might take a while, transformation is coming. The caterpillar yields itself to God and waits for the transformation to take place.

Monday Is Still Coming: Life-Changing Reflections Beyond Sunday comes at a Kairos moment (opportune time) in the life of the Christian church. Reverend Tracy La'Nai Clark, in her book, helps us shine a light on ourselves, reconnect to God, yield ourselves into God's hands, and allow the transforming power of the Holy Spirit to change our lives.

Reverend Clark, throughout her written reflections, calls on us to have caterpillar faith which will give us "strength in your weak moments," to know that, even when we are hanging upside down in a cocoon, we can say "I'm in a blessed place."

ACKNOWLEDGEMENTS

I'd like to thank God, who is my Savior, Deliverer, and Comforter, for the opportunity to write this book. This book is the result of many people that have divinely stepped into my life through the years. I am the sum total of those that have poured into me from the beginning to this day.

I am grateful for the late Dr. Wade Richmond, my first pastor, who baptized me at the age of eleven at St. John's Baptist Church in Far Rockaway, New York, who poured into me by preaching the gospel of Jesus Christ with power in season and out.

I am grateful for Dr. M. Louis Lacey, pastor of the Children of God Victory Tabernacle, Richmond, Virginia. His demonstration of love, patience, and understanding, while serving as the church's musician, enabled me to receive Jesus Christ as my Lord and Savior under his ministry.

I am blessed to have a pastor, spiritual mother, and friend in Rev. Linda D. Stevens, who has encouraged me, prayed for, and has always been a supporter in all my endeavors, who, in addition to my sweet mother, imparted the importance of a strong prayer life. For that, I am grateful.

To the friends of Westwood Baptist Church, Richmond, Virginia, that nurtured a young musician and preacher growing in the Lord. To each who participated in some way in my spiritual journey, I am thankful.

To the disciples of New Life Empowerment Temple where God allowed me to pastor, I am eternally grateful. You allowed me to always be transparent, bringing everyday life circumstances to the text. Thank you for letting me be me.

My family has always been an integral part of my life. My parents, John and Brenda Clark, demonstrated the love of God before me, the importance of a strong faith, a consistent prayer life, and integrity. It is because of them that I am.

To my grandparents, Claude and Lucy Huntley, Charlie and Annie Mae Byrd, and Theodore Clark, thank you for imparting a love for the Lord, music and family.

I thank God for my loving brother, Travis, and sister-in-love, Angel. Your excitement about this project was very encouraging. To Kennedy and Gavin, thank you for being the best niece and nephew an aunt could ever ask for.

Finally, I wish to thank Melva McGlen and Books 2 Business Publishing for, not only their excitement about this project, but their ability to capture the essence of my vision in such a professional manner from start to finish. Thank you.

TABLE OF CONTENTS

INTRODUCTION

Monday is Still Coming: Life-Changing Reflections Beyond Sunday is a compilation of conversational-style messages intended to bring insight and encouragement through the scriptures, as well as facilitate an inner dialogue about life's everyday circumstances. Life happens fast. Monday is inevitable.

This book was born because of the breakdown that takes place between Sunday and Monday for many believers. I've seen people get excited about the spirited, well-written, and perfectly executed sermons on Sunday, but, somehow, by Monday, they've totally forgotten what they've heard! They've become defeated, depressed, and despondent all over again. Life has thrown them lemons, and they've forgotten how to make lemonade on Monday! I couldn't understand the disconnect.

The answer came when I heard a well-known pastor in an interview say, "People are being churched and not changed." When you're churched, you hear a message and say, "That was powerful" or "The pastor preached today," but then Monday comes. When people change, it is usually because they have internalized and applied the text. At some point, there must be some application to what is heard and what our response to life is going to be beyond Sunday. We all have or will experience suffering, disappointment, or just life's stuff. We can't always control what happens to us, but we *can* control our response.

Tracy La'Nai Clark

This book contains messages based around scripture, each with stories and illustrations meant to expound on the text. It is my intent that, as you navigate through each reflection, you will be able to equip, empower, and encourage yourself as you enjoy compelling messages, each with complementary daily prayers to get you *Beyond Sunday*.

DAY 1

WHAT IN HELL ARE YOU TALKING ABOUT?

Jonah 1:17, 2:1-2 (King James Version): *Now the Lord had prepared a great fish to swallow up Jonah. And Jonah was in the belly of the fish three days and three nights. Then Jonah prayed unto the Lord his God out of the fish's belly, And said, I cried by reason of mine affliction unto the Lord, and he heard me; out of the belly of hell cried I, and thou heardest my voice.*

Oftentimes, we look around, and things seem deplorable and devastating. Sickness, disease, and limited finances consume our thoughts. Life stuff has no rhyme or reason for happening. And then, when it happens, why does it seem to happen to you? Life can be hell. But here you are saved and sanctified, and hell is coming at you full force. Being saved doesn't mean that hell stops. As a matter of fact, hell kicks up a notch because you're saved. Just because you have been renewed in your thinking doesn't mean hell stops. Hell is on assignment for your mind. Hell is on assignment for your life. Hell wants to attach itself to anything and everything that is important to you. Hell wants your anointing. As a matter of fact, hell wants you! Hell can be a place and an emotion. The pit. The lowest place. The hurtful place. The place that is the opposite of all that is good. The place of devastation. The place where misery resides.

When you're going through hell, you need the word of God planted in your mouth. When you're going through hell, you need to be able to articulate what *thus saith the Lord* about a matter. When you're going through hell, you need to be able to speak God's promises about your situation, rather than the situation itself.

When you're sick, what you want to be talking about is what God says about you getting well. When you're broke, what does God say about being wealthy? The word of God is going to keep you as you go through hell. What you talk about when you're in hell is just as important as what you talk about when you're not.

Because you have established a relationship with God when you are in the pit of misery, when you're dealing with depression, when you're dealing with anxiety or loneliness, you should have a word that you can stand on. When you understand the power of God's promises over your life, while you're going through something, you have enough of the word of God to keep your mind in perfect peace.

In this text, Jonah had been given an assignment from God to go to Nineveh, so he might preach against the wickedness there, but Jonah decided that the assignment was not important enough for him to be obedient. Well, the truth of the matter is, there are consequences to disobedience.

Deuteronomy 28:15 (KJV): *But it shall come to pass, if thou wilt not hearken unto the voice of the Lord thy God, to observe to do all his commandments and his statutes which I command thee this day; that all these curses shall come upon thee, and overtake thee.*

And so now Jonah finds himself fleeing from the assignment of God to Tarshish, on a ship, in the middle of the sea. The King James Version describes the sea as "tempestuous." In other words, it was turbulent, wild, and conflicting.

There are several things we can learn from this text. When you disobey and try to escape the will of God, things around you, that may have been calm, will become raging because you don't belong there.

Secondly, when you're going through hell, everyone is not going to want to go with you, just because you've decided to be disobedient. The text shows us that, after the shipmen threw Jonah overboard, the seas became calm. Then, the Lord prepared a great fish to swallow him up. In other words, Jonah was in hell.

Then Jonah prayed unto the Lord his God, the text says. When you have a relationship with God, what you do ordinarily will become a natural occurrence when you're in hell. When you're in hell, prayer is the key! Praying to God during your time in hell will bring, not only comfort, but direction.

Not only did Jonah pray, but he cried. The reason why many of us don't receive deliverance from a thing is because we haven't cried out to God. The text says, *I cried by reason of my affliction...and He heard me.* When your own affliction causes you to cry out, God hears you. My question to you today is, are you crying out to God? When you're going through hell, what in hell are you talking about?

Some time ago, I went to a nail shop, and as I usually do, I struck up a light conversation with the nail technician, who was servicing me. After we exchanged pleasantries, I asked her if she had come to the States to go to school or for another reason. She responded, "You're not really interested in hearing my story, are you?"

I responded, "Sure. I would love to hear your story."

It turns out her family were refugees from Vietnam, and they stole away in a refugee boat. They were called "boat people." From 1978 to 1995, Vietnamese refugee camps were alive and well.

She said, while her family was out in the middle of the ocean, water started coming into their boat. They almost drowned. The sweltering sun beat on their faces by day, scorching their lips and skin. But even during this tumultuous life event, for some reason, they kept saying, "Someone is going to see us." Her family knew that they had to get to America.

They spent eleven days in the open sea. "It was hell," she said, but their declaration remained the same on the eleventh day as it was on the first day: "Someone is going to see us."

Don't you know, when God wants you to be seen, you will be seen? He will set everything in motion, just for you, so He can get glory out of a situation. Some folks try to be seen before God is ready for them to be visible! We try to put things in motion and people in place, but it's not God's timing. God wants to get the glory out of our lives through and in every situation.

And so it was, on the eleventh day, a big Norwegian ship was on the seas, in the middle of a great storm, en route to the United States. Someone on that ship saw something in the ocean. In the middle of the raging seas and onslaught of winds, someone saw them, and they were saved and brought to the United States.

What am I saying? God sees you in the midst of your hell! Jonah had been in the belly of the whale for three days and three nights. But when God has a plan for your life, even in your disobedience, you will get to your predestined place. When God has a plan for your life, you may go through some tempestuous times, like Jonah. You may even try to run from God's plan, but because it's God's plan, you will get to the other side.

This woman's testimony blessed my life because she had been in the ocean, essentially in the middle of nowhere, for eleven days. She said, "I don't know where I was to this day, but I know where I ended up." Glory to God! She said, "I know I could have been dead, but God sent a miracle! God sent help!" At the end of her story, she sang "The Star-Spangled Banner." At this point, I thought I was being punked or, perhaps, she was delirious from the chemicals in the nail salon. But God reminded me that she had arrived in the United States following an eleven-day journey on a boat. It was hell! But somebody saw them!

What God told me was "Tracy, if you were in hell like she was for eleven days and were able to tell your story of being a refugee many years later, now that you had finally gotten to the place where you'd set out to get, you, too, would be singing 'Oh, say can you see, by the dawn's early light, what so proudly we hailed at the twilight's last gleaming.' We take life for granted! We take freedom for granted! If it had not been for the Lord, who was on our side, where would we be?

At the conclusion of her song, she looked at me and smiled and said, "Thank you for listening to my story. I'm singing because I have a job. I'm singing because I'm alive."

God sees each of us, whether we're in the belly of a great fish or in our hell moments. If we just keep the faith, remember His word, and cry out to Him, nothing is impossible.

Dear Father, when life seems to be so overwhelming and feels like we're in hell, help us to remember that you, El Roi, see us. Thank you for your saving grace. May we continue to profess your promises. In Jesus' name, Amen.

DAY 2

THIS IS THE DAY

Psalm 118:24 (KJV): *This is the day which the LORD hath made; we will rejoice and be glad in it.*

This scripture is, perhaps, the most commonly quoted scripture on a Sunday in every church between the hours of ten o'clock and eleven o'clock. It is a scripture that is often appropriated for the onset of a worship service; almost without thought, it is said, but few who hear this scripture are able to live out its true meaning beyond Sunday morning. Somewhere along the line, our thinking has converged upon the precipice of the ideology that the reference to this day only means Sunday. As a result, we freely give the enemy a foothold on Monday, and this scriptural reference is no longer applicable. The text says: This is the day. So it can apply to any day we choose to rejoice.

The enemy is not threatened, in the least, by the fact that this is the day the Lord has made, but he becomes excited when the latter part of that text becomes easier and easier to get the body of believers off track. He becomes excited about the part that states: I will rejoice and be glad in it. And so here comes another day, a day that brings situations, a day that brings trials. Here comes that day, a day that just brought out the worst in me. A day where all seems lost. A day that feels overwhelming, and a day that brings nothing but tears. Here comes that day. A day where nobody understands me. A day where I can't make myself understood. Here comes that day! And somehow, in the middle of that day, I'm expected to say,

11

"This is the day that the Lord has made. I will rejoice and be glad in it."

What's going on in your life should have no effect on your testimony. You should still be able to rejoice by virtue of who God is in your life, not what your situation is in your life. Sometimes, you've got to think about how God has blessed you. Sometimes, you've got to think about His goodness. Think about the last time He brought you out of a situation. Think about how He made a way, when no way seemed possible. Think about when you were down to your last, and then someone, out of nowhere, blessed you. Think about how He's blessed your children. Think about how He's kept your mind.

To rejoice is to celebrate the very idea of something that is or is to come. Because the mind is so powerful, we can cause ourselves to be in a constant celebratory state simply by being there already in our mind. This text reminds us that we need not focus our attention on the things of yesterday because yesterday is gone or on the things of tomorrow because tomorrow is not here. Instead, we should rejoice in this day because this is the day that the Lord has made. If you can't get excited about anything else, get excited about this day, this moment. You're alive on this day. God kept you through last night. For some folks, they can only celebrate the idea of going to heaven, but every day, they're absolutely miserable, miserable when they wake up, miserable during the day, miserable when they come home. Their children see them miserable. Their spouses see them miserable. Their coworkers see misery written all over them. They look in the mirror, and all they see is misery. So rejoicing is far from their radar. It's easy to get excited about heaven. We can always rejoice because we are going to a place where there will be no more crying, no more sickness, no more bills, no more dying.

We get excited about heaven, but it's difficult to rejoice when things are trying. If you can only worship God when things are good, then your worship is one-sided, so this scripture says: "This is the day!" This is the day I will.

To will oneself means I may not feel like it situations may not be ideal, but there's something about my will that says, "Despite my circumstances, despite my finances, despite the layoff, despite this separation, despite the divorce, despite the diagnosis, despite how things may look, despite all that I have lost, despite all the attacks, I will rejoice!" In other words, I make myself! I declare it in my spirit. I will rejoice and be glad in it. When you make up in your mind that you will rejoice this day, you can't put yourself in the company of people who like to discuss your yesterday. They want to talk up yesterday. Yesterday was important to them. Yesterday can mean anything before this day. Yesterday could be last week, last month, or last year. When we allow ourselves to focus on yesterday, we don't make room for God in our today. We need to declare and decree the Word of God so that our spirit can hear it differently. When we declare, "This is the day that the Lord has made, I will rejoice and be glad in it," then that lets me know that our rejoicing is predicated upon what God made. In other words, God, in the face of the enemy, will make some things happen for your life, and then you rejoice. God can make you the head and not the tail. Rejoice and be glad in that. Make you a lender and not a borrower. Make you above and not beneath. Make you more than a conqueror. Make you eat from the fat of the land. Make you have abundant life. Rejoice and be glad in that. Make goodness and mercy follow you! Sometimes, in the face of adversity, we've got to tell the enemy, "Here comes this day, and I plan on rejoicing and being glad in it! No weapon that is formed against me shall keep me from rejoicing in this day. This day, I am reconciled with Christ. This day, I am justified by faith. This day, I am victorious in all that I set out to do. This day, I am free from condemnation. This is the day I am drawing closer to God than ever before. Nothing and no one shall separate me from the love of Christ in this day. This is the day that the Lord has made. I will rejoice and be glad in it!"

Dear Father, no matter what the day may bring, I will rejoice and be glad in it. You are a great God, and You deserve all honor and glory each and every day. In Jesus' name, Amen.

DAY 3

A FAR COUNTRY

Luke 15:11–15, 20 (KJV): *And he said, A certain man had two sons: 12And the younger of them said to his father, Father, give me the portion of goods that falleth to me. And he divided unto them his living. 13And not many days after the younger son gathered all together, and took his journey into a far country, and there wasted his substance with riotous living. 14And when he had spent all, there arose a mighty famine in that land; and he began to be in want. 15And he went and joined himself to a citizen of that country; and he sent him into his fields to feed swine. 16And he would fain have filled his belly with the husks that the swine did eat: and no man gave unto him. 17And when he came to himself, he said, how many hired servants of my father's have bread enough and to spare, and I perish with hunger! 18I will arise and go to my father, and will say unto him, Father, I have sinned against heaven, and before thee, 19And am no more worthy to be called thy son: make me as one of thy hired servants. 20And he arose and came to his father. But when he was yet a great way off, his father saw him, and had compassion, and ran, and fell on his neck, and kissed him.*

This text has a myriad of messages packed into it. I have always heard it from the perspective of each person within the text. I have heard it from the perspective of the elder brother. Other perspectives have been on the forgiving and celebratory father. Then, there are others from the perspective of the repentant son. But I want us to consider the perspective of the place this text calls a far country. A far country is not just a place but a state of being. A state of consciousness. A position.

A far country – where there are no rules.

A far country – where there's no covering.

A far country – where there's nobody looking over my shoulder.

A far country – where anything goes.

A far country – the place that will take every dime you've ever had.

A far country – the place where your thoughts are never on the Father, until you have nothing left.

We have overlooked the importance and the transformative power of the far country en route to getting to the party! We want to hear about the father running to his son. We want to hear about the fatted calf. Tell us more about the robe and the ring, and what about the shoes that were placed on his feet? But nobody wants to hear about what happened in the far country. The son says in this pericope, "Give me what's mine now." When there is an urgency to receive prematurely what's rightfully yours, you set yourself up for the consequences that come with that. Then, the text says he joined himself with a citizen of that country. In other words, he connected to other folks. When you unite yourself with others outside of your father's kingdom, you gradually personify one who has no authority and one who does not understand his place in God. When you unite with someone from another place, in this case, the far country, that which is in you will be misused or abused because the gift that is in you is not for that place but for the place you left. The text says: And he sent him into the fields to feed swine. When you unite in the far country, you may have to do a job that you were never ordained to do!

Sometimes, we have to go through the far country and be tolerated in order to get to the place where God would have us to be celebrated! I'm sure all kinds of folks were in the far country, living riotously, as the text says. But what we fail to realize is that change happened in a far country. Let's not be so quick to discount those in a far country. We, too, were once in a far country before we came into relationship with our Father. When we were in a far country, we thought we had everything we needed. When we were in a far country, we thought everybody was on the same page. But had it not been for the far country, this son wouldn't have known he was lost. Outside of the kingdom, you have to live like those with no authority. Within the kingdom, you have benefits. Outside of the kingdom you're like any other citizen. Within the kingdom, there is excess. Outside of the kingdom, there is famine. Within the kingdom, there is sonship and relationship. God reminds us, through this text, that there are some people in our lives that are in a far country. But as soon as the famine comes, they'll be returning to God, and when they do, it is our responsibility to receive them with open arms; for we, too, were once in a far country, and God received us unto himself.

Dear Father, thank you for the experiences of the far country. Because of that season in our lives, it has brought us back to you. Help us, likewise, to receive others, who may have gone astray. Amen.

DAY 4

EXAMINE YOURSELF

1 Corinthians 11:28-32 (KJV): *But let a man examine himself, and so let him eat of that bread, and drink of that cup. For he that eateth and drinketh unworthily, eateth and drinketh damnation to himself, not discerning the Lord's body. For this cause many are weak and sickly among you, and many sleep. For if we would judge ourselves, we should not be judged. But when we are judged, we are chastened of the Lord, that we should not be condemned with the world.*

We are at a critical time, not just in the world, but in the body of Christ. The gospel is, somehow, being downplayed, and being better entrepreneurs is taking precedence over being better believers. Somehow, salvation, deliverance, and making disciples are on the low-end of the proverbial totem pole, and marital and relationship tips come in at a strong number one.

Where are those who still desire to hear about the things of God and His kingdom? Where are those who know the power of prayer and will hold on to the horns of the altar until a change comes? Where are those that desire a deeper understanding of the Gospel? Where are those that understand the importance of repentance and forgiveness? Are there still mothers that wail in their prayer closets for the lives of the dying children in our communities? Is there anyone crying in the midnight hour for the incarcerated? Who's going out in the streets at two o'clock and three o'clock in the morning, ministering to the prostitute and the heroin addict? All of us, at some point, need to fully examine ourselves. True examination of oneself, although a humbling experience, allows us to make necessary changes for the greater good, knowing that it's about His kingdom and not our own.

This corrective and instructive letter from Paul to the church at Corinth was relative to the feast that would often accompany communion. Many would gorge themselves on food and drink while others went without. This text presents to the church a need to examine themselves, or rather, do a heart check. Were they coming to unite in community over a meal and acknowledge the Christ or just to eat? Examining ourselves is critical as a believer. At some point in time, we will be faced with acknowledging the truth about why we do what we do.

I enjoy the approach of Dr. Iyanla Vanzant on Fix My Life as she deals with people in crises. What I admire most about this show is how she listens intently to her clients' stories and observes the finger-pointing of others in their lives that has caused them great angst. After hearing their stories, she firmly and matter-of-factly interrupts them and says, "What is your part in all of this?" And then she sends them away to a solitary place, a place to reflect, to journal, and just to sit with themselves in their issue. And upon their return, she begins the process of healing, which is at the intersection of their truth and reality. Their truth is often the stories that they have rehearsed in their own minds as to how things are; however, the reality is how things really are. True healing begins at the understanding of reality. What am I saying? There is a story that is the truth, and for others, there is a story that sounds better to our ears, that is easier to swallow, but the truth will have us examining ourselves in order to understand our part in a scenario. God desires a true healing for His people. God desires that we examine ourselves.

As we move toward and in the things of God, may we be mindful of the importance of always humbling ourselves and examining our motives. May we keep our hands busy for the kingdom of God, knowing that there are still many who have not come to this Savior. As we examine ourselves fully, may we be more be concerned about the dying souls in our world than we are about what church they belong to. Let us examine ourselves in all we do, so our journey in Him is more fruitful, more faithful, more prayerful, and more in tune with His voice.

Dear Father, thank you for reminding us to examine ourselves, so you can be glorified in all that we do. Help us to reconcile any areas of our lives that don't please you. In Jesus' name, Amen.

DAY 5

TALK ABOUT YOUR BUT

2 Kings 5:1 (KJV): *Now Naaman, captain of the host of the king of Syria, was a great man with his master, and honorable, because by him the LORD had given deliverance unto Syria: he was also a mighty man in valor, but he was a leper.*

In 2016, the music industry lost a musical genius — Prince Rogers Nelson. With an impressive repertoire, this man influenced the music industry in such a way that, to this day, we can still sing the songs he wrote back in the seventies and eighties verbatim. It's amazing that, after an extensive investigation, they concluded that he died of an apparent drug overdose, so now history has to be recorded to read, he was a musical genius, *but* he died of a drug overdose. My question to us today is, what is your *but*, and can you talk about it?

The church, just like the hospital, should be a place for the sick to come and get well, for the broken-hearted to come and get mended. The church should be the place where the unloved can come and receive love. The church should be a place where, when the world has blocked them out and cast them aside, the unloved can feel a part of something. So, if that is the case, then why is it so convenient for people to recall one's accomplishments while tagging on a *but* at the end of that person's life resume? Whether they know it or not, God is in *that* place. The place that seems ugly. The place that seems unmentionable. The place that seems undesirable. That's the place where God begins His work. His delivering power. His salvific power. It's in that place, where God begins his work in us. We replay the *buts* in people's lives, notwithstanding the power of God to do a new thing in us. Perhaps you've heard the stories: He was a pastor, a leader, and a husband, *but* he had a mistress. She was a politician, a wife, and a mother to three beautiful children, *but* she had an alcohol addiction. They were a power couple; their children were in Ivy League schools, *but* the husband lived a double life. He had scholarships from the top universities, a job lined up before he even graduated, *but* he sold ecstasy out of his backpack during school hours. She was a wonderful dancer; she loved the Lord, *but* she had a child out of wedlock.

The church gets stuck on the *but* and magnifies the accomplishments before the *but*, so we boast about the accomplishments yet sit in the seat of the scornful while recalling the unimaginable, the ugly thing. Yet that's the place where God is! I wrestled with this text because it can be considered a text that speaks to the account of a healing miracle or one that highlights his accomplishments, despite his disease. We all have a *but* in our lives.

Naaman was a leader. The text says: *Naaman was a man of honor.* Naaman had great nobility. We knew about his leadership and his successes. Then, the text tags on that small three letter word — *but*. But he was a leper.

We all have a *but* in our lives. This is the place where humility resides. This place, when or if uncovered, should bring us down a few notches and humble us. This is the place where God has been or is working some things out in us. The *but* serves as a reminder, telling us that, without God, we would be nowhere. Naaman had earned the love and respect of his king. Yet, with all his strength and might, Naaman suffered from the dreadful disease of leprosy. Naaman suffered from pride and faulty expectations. He wanted a quick fix and special treatment.

For some folks, having a *but* in their lives presents a form of entitlement, and for others, it positions them for a healing and a breakthrough.

Perhaps, Naaman is not the only one with leprosy. Sometimes, the church can be leprous. Leprosy, depending upon the victim, may remain localized, or it may spread. Leprosy causes nerve destruction in the infected areas. It causes the victim to lose his sense of feeling in those areas. It is this loss of feeling that poses one of the greatest dangers to the leper. If he hurts himself in one of these areas, he may not recognize his injury or the severity of it until it becomes infected or has infected other parts of his body. Sometimes, the church can be leprous.

It's an amazing thing that the Hebrew meaning of the name Naaman is "pleasant, pleasantness, beautiful, agreeable, or delightful." This is everything that Naaman was not until God stepped in!

Naaman was a man who had a first-class ticket to society. He was the Colin Powell of his day, a hero to his king, as well as the nation. Naaman was the man who had everything, *but* he had leprosy.

In this season of your life, perhaps consider talking about your *but*. What has God healed you from? Delivered you from? Pulled you out of? Could it be that, if and when you talk about your *but*, God can be glorified and someone's life edified, just because they've heard your story? The Bible says, in Revelation 12:11 (KJV): *And they overcame him by the blood of the Lamb, and by the word of their testimony; and they loved not their lives unto the death.* God has only the best in mind for His children. God can bless you, use you, and set you up for greatness, in spite of your *but*. Consider that part and watch God work!

Dear Father, thank you for loving us in and through those ugly, undesirable, and unmentionable places in our lives that we don't talk about, and for allowing us to be new creatures in Christ. Amen.

Mom's Memos

ARE YOU CONNECTED?

One evening, my husband and I decided to take a train into Manhattan. We ran and got on the train, got comfortable, and sat, waiting for the train to move. A conductor came up to us and said, "You all will have to move forward, if you are going anywhere."

"Why?" we asked. "We are comfortable here."

"Well, this car is not connected to anything that will take you anywhere."

Are you sitting in a church that is not connected, where the gospel of Jesus Christ is not being preached? Are you even going anywhere?

DAY 6

CHANGE YOUR MIND CHANGE YOUR WAYS

Romans 8:5-8 (KJV): *For they that are after the flesh do mind the things of the flesh; but they that are after the Spirit the things of the Spirit. For to be carnally minded is death; but to be spiritually minded is life and peace. Because the carnal mind is enmity against God: for it is not subject to the law of God, neither indeed can be. So then they that are in the flesh cannot please God.*

In What's So Amazing About Grace?, Phillip Yancey wrote, "All too often the church holds up a mirror reflecting back the society around it, rather than a window revealing a different way." When the church holds up a mirror to itself, it doesn't always see God, it sees the world! The church is running amuck, seeking new ways to bring people to the house of God. The Word of God no longer works, so the church does things that have nothing to do with His Word, so you don't get offended, but, at least, you can come in the house! When that happens, the thing that was used to get these people into the house can't be maintained to keep them there, so they leave and go somewhere else.

The church is in perilous times. Romans 12:2 reminds us about conforming to this world. When we conform, we no longer exhibit Godly fruit. Our character does not imitate that which pleases God. We are not as compassionate or as patient as we could be. When we conform to this world, we become self-centered and are not loyal in our commitments. When we conform to the world, it doesn't tell us when it's changing. Comparatively speaking, while you were trying to keep up with the world and buy CDs, the world changed and is now listening to digital playlists! When you decided to start taking pictures of you and your friends with a Polaroid, the world started taking selfies with its iPhone. Now in some of our communities, you've gone out to buy a perm to straighten your hair, and the world went to the hair store and bought weaves! The moment you started wearing weaves, the world decided to go natural!

In much the same way, the church is trying to keep up with the world, but it can't because the world keeps changing the standard. The church should not have to conform to the world's standards; instead, it should set the standards for the world. The church universal has become a spiritual building operating in carnality. Therefore, our text says: The carnal mind is enmity against God. It does not say it is opposed to God, but it is positive enmity. It is not an enmity, but enmity itself! It is not corrupt, but corruption. It is not rebellious; it is rebellion. It is not wicked; it is wickedness itself. And so, this scripture tells us to be carnally minded is enmity against God. A carnal-minded person has a grave dislike for the things of God. This scripture, also, reveals to us that being spiritually minded pleases God and will lead to life and peace.

When you are carnally minded, you cater to the appetites and impulses of your flesh. Carnally minded is thinking and doing what is right in one's own eyes, not what is right in God's eyes. To be carnally minded means to be facts-minded, emotions-driven, and controlled by natural circumstances. To be carnally minded means you have a mindset that is contrary to God, His Word, and His will for your life. The carnal mind is always focused on the problem. Carnal-minded thinkers are always victims and never victors.

Then, there is the spiritually minded being who is led by the Spirit of God. A spiritual mindset is nourished by intimate times with God and meditation on the Word of God, prayer, fasting, listening to God, and listening for God. Psalm 42:1-2 (KJV): As the deer panteth after the water brooks, so panteth my soul after thee, O God. My soul thirsteth for God, for the living God. Being spiritually minded means you have given the Holy Spirit control over your thinking. Spiritually minded folks wait on God for answers. They do not give God the question and the answer! A spiritually minded person overflows with love, joy, peace, patience, kindness, goodness, gentleness, faithfulness, and self-control of the Spirit. A spiritual mindset is the mind of Christ in operation, no longer dependent on human wisdom, insights, and reasoning. There are times, even in the church, when we have relied too much on our intellect and human reasoning, so much so that we've not welcomed the Holy Spirit into the picture.

The truth of the matter is you are either being carnally minded or spiritually minded because there is no "in-between." You either have the mindset of the natural, carnal world, or you are taking on the mind of Christ! Carnal words cause us to become wearier, more hopeless, more helpless, and more anxious, while spiritual words build up, edify, cause our faith to rise, cause our hope to leap with expectancy, and cause our joy to break forth. The carnal mind uses people and opportunities for its own purpose and self-value. There is something that happens when you've decided not to do something for somebody with a carnal mind; there is a mood, a new disposition, either exposed or internalized, that comes upon this person. But when you function under the mind of Christ, you don't have to see it before you believe it. You don't have to understand it before you accept it. You don't have to be right. Under the mind of Christ, you don't worry about fairness. You can accept correction without mumbling under your breath. Under the mind of Christ, you wait on God. Under the mind of Christ, you take responsibility and repent. When you operate under the mind of Christ, your "self" can die daily. When you change your mind and live according to the spirit, God is in control.

I submit to you today that we will be more cognizant about taking on the mind of Christ! We will strive to live according to the spirit. Because we have the mind of Christ, His favor will find us. Because we have the mind of Christ, God's blessings will overtake us. Because we have the mind of Christ, purpose will carry us. Because we have the mind of Christ, wealth will see us and His stripes will heal us. Because we have the mind of Christ, His peace will overtake us. When we change our minds, we can ultimately change our ways. God has great things in store for us. Won't you consider being spiritually minded today?

Dear Father, enable us to take on the mind of Christ, in all our endeavors, as we strive to please you. In Jesus' name, Amen.

DAY 7

I FORGOT

Psalm 103:1-5 (KJV): *Bless the* LORD, *O my soul: and all that is within me, bless his holy name* ²*Bless the* LORD, *O my soul, and forget not all his benefits:*³ *Who forgiveth all thine iniquities; who healeth all thy diseases;*⁴ *Who redeemeth thy life from destruction; who crowneth thee with lovingkindness and tender mercies;*⁵ *Who satisfieth thy mouth with good things; so that thy youth is renewed like the eagle's.*

Have we, somehow, become an if then community of believers? In other words, if God does this, then I can bless the Lord. If God gets my children out of trouble, then I can bless the Lord. If God can pay this mortgage, then I can bless the Lord. If God can heal this lump, then I can bless the Lord. The church has made blessing God directly proportional to that which God does or will do. And so, when God is not needed, it appears that God cannot be blessed. God is waiting to be blessed, not because of what He can do, but just because of who He is! This is the beginning of authentic worship! When we can bless the Lord without prompting, prodding, or reminding, therein lies the authentic worship, the secret place.

The text goes on to say: Bless the Lord, O my soul: and all that is within me, bless his holy name. **Your ability to bless the Lord is within you!** Waiting for a pastor, a preacher, or another church leader to get you to the place of blessing the Lord happens when you don't realize that what you need is what you came with. The praise that's already in you came with you! You have the ability to bless God because he is already within you. My external circumstances should never dictate what's going on in me because what's in me should always be blessing God. We can give God an "in spite of" praise because, in spite of what's going on around us, God deserves to be blessed! In spite of what it looks like, in spite of what it appears to be, in spite of what it feels like, God deserves to be blessed.

If you just had a glimpse of what God kept you from, you'd come before God with your praise! If you had any idea that, last night, someone was on their way into your home, but God encamped angels all around your home and kept them from breaking in, you'd be blessing God! Bless the Lord, not because of what you know but because of what you don't know! We need to enter the presence of God prepared to praise God. Your Bible declares, in Psalm 100:4 (KJV): Enter his gates with thanksgiving, and into his courts with praise: be thankful unto him, and bless his name.

The text goes on to say (Psalm 103:2 KJV): Bless the Lord, O my soul, and forget not all his benefits. **Your ability to bless the Lord is predicated upon your remembering his benefits.** The benefits of God should keep you in a posture of remembering your history with God. In other words, if He did it before, He can do it again! And so, this scripture is proving and declaring that there are benefits in not forgetting! We all forget. Our daily lives are inundated with a myriad of thoughts, both trivial and significant; however, there is a differentiation with what one forgets and what one chooses to remember.

We forget that bad relationship, but we remember that one who stole our heart.

We forget to take the trash out, but we remember the one who didn't.

We forget to pay a light bill, but we remember the moment night falls.

We forget when we have to give a sacrificial offering, but we remember that we have to buy tickets for our vacation in June.

The difference between what we forget and what we remember depends largely on whether it is a reward or a benefit. Children will forget to clean their rooms, but when you attach a reward to the task, there's value in remembering. Johnny may get twenty dollars for taking out the trash, so you only have to tell him once. Susie has to clean her room and wash the dishes, but she doesn't get a dime, so she conveniently forgets. Forgetting has no benefits. Remembering does! There are no consequences to forgetting. Therefore, a worship experience within any assembly on any given day can be fruitful and memorable based upon how many people remember. Even though it is a cliché, the phrase "We had church today" is no longer predicated upon what you did, what was preached, or who sang, but what you remembered once you got there!

Your life is dependent on His benefits. Forgiveness of sin in this text is the very first benefit. If we bless God for no other reason, it should be because sin has caused us to stumble, and when we stumble, we believe we can't bless the Lord. The job of the enemy is to keep the saints of God in a constant war within themselves, helping them to remember what they did. David is saying, once you command your soul to bless God, your sins are forgiven! People of God stifle their worship because they feel like they don't have a right to worship God after all they've done. The devil is a liar! It's not about what you've done, but what God has done on your behalf. The scripture asks: Who forgives your iniquities? (Psalm 103:3 NKJV). You can bless God for that. You can't give God what He is due because you're too bound up being concerned about who or what did you wrong and why. The most confused moments in your walk are probably the moments that you spend in worship because the enemy attacks your thoughts right in the middle of your worship and brings about condemnation and distraction to the point where you can't even lift holy hands. But if you ever get yourself to the place where you can push through and bless the Lord, you will be opening the door for a continuous flow of benefits. The text shows us that, if you bless the Lord, He'll forgive your sin. If you bless the Lord, He'll heal you. If you bless the Lord, He'll redeem you. If you bless the Lord, he'll satisfy you.

When you command your soul to bless God, the windows of heaven begin to open and pour out blessings. When you command your soul to bless the Lord, God is glorified, and hell is horrified. When you command your soul to bless the Lord, Satan has got to back up and yield to what the Lord says. When you command your soul to bless the Lord, you can be free from condemnation.

When you command your soul to bless the Lord, you realize that you are the elect of God. When you command your soul to bless the Lord, you understand that you are the righteousness of God. The Bible says: Bless the lord, O my soul, and forget not all his benefits.

Don't forget that he loves you, loves you enough to heal diseases. Cancer is not difficult for him to heal. AIDS is not hard for him to cure. Diabetes is just a simple thing in the hands of God. Multiple Sclerosis (MS) is just a small thing in the hands of Jehovah Rophe. Don't forget that he loves you, loves you enough to redeem your life from destruction. Don't forget that he loves you, loves you enough to crown you with His mercy. Lamentations 3:23 (KJV) says: It is of the Lord's mercies that we are not consumed, because his compassions fail not. They are new every morning: great is thy faithfulness. Don't forget that He loves you, loves you enough to satisfy you with good things. Satisfy you with advancements. Satisfy you with raises and bonuses. Satisfy you with favor with creditors. Satisfy you with writing abilities. Satisfy you with visions and dreams. Satisfy you with increased income. Bless the Lord, not because of what He can do, but because of who He is! Bless the Lord because your ability to bless God is within you. Bless the Lord because your ability to bless God is predicated upon your remembering. Bless the Lord because your life is dependent upon his benefits.

Dear Father, forgive us for forgetting how good you are and thank you for being a good Father, who blesses us with benefits, despite how we may bless you. Amen.

DAY 8

I'm In A Blessed Place

Psalm 1:1-6 (KJV): *Blessed is the man that walketh not in the counsel of the ungodly, nor standeth in the way of sinners, nor sitteth in the seat of the scornful. But his delight is in the law of the Lord; and in his law doth he meditate day and night. And he shall be like a tree planted by the rivers of water, that bringeth forth his fruit in his season; his leaf also shall not wither; and whatsoever he doeth shall prosper. The ungodly are not so: but are like the chaff which the wind driveth away. Therefore the ungodly shall not stand in the judgment, nor sinners in the congregation of the righteous. For the Lord knoweth the way of the righteous: but the way of the ungodly shall perish.*

Are you blessed? Do you speak as if you're blessed? Do you walk in the authority of one that is blessed? Are you listening to or reading the Word of God that reinforces how blessed you are?

According to this text, there are two types of people. There is the blessed man, and then there's the ungodly. The blessed man cannot walk in the counsel of the ungodly. The blessed man has distinct characteristics of godliness (see verse 3). The ungodly man is like the chaff (husks, seeds, pods, and shells) where the wind drives it away.

Aren't we all desiring to be a blessed man or woman of God? According to this text, there is a blessed person, a blessed time, and a blessed place. The blessed person is the godly. The blessed time is day and night. The blessed place is planted.

When you are planted, you will see fruit. When you are planted, your roots are strong, and nothing can shake you. Nothing can move you, regardless of the season. When you are planted, you yield fruit. When you are planted with strong roots, you yield fruit in your set season. But when you are not planted, nothing grows.

Being in a blessed place comes as a direct result of each being in tandem with the other — being planted and bringing forth fruit. In other words, fruit is a manifestation of life. Fruit lets me know that something is at work within that tree. Fruit is not sporadic or mutant, but fruit, in the right atmosphere and with the right nurturing, will always yield in its season. When a tree that was planted does not bring forth fruit, then there are one of two problems — something is wrong with the soil, or the tree has been infected. So it is in the natural, so it is in the spirit. When there is an infection, it usually happens from the inside out. So, for a long time, you might see what looks like a healthy tree from the outside, but it could be slowly dying on the inside. When there is infection, there is stunted growth. When there is infection, there is decay. When there is infection, there are growths near wounds, near the hurt places, near the unforeseen places. But you would never know a tree has been infected or even tampered with until it's time to bear fruit! So it is in the natural, so it is in the spirit.

My father had several fruit trees in his backyard in North Carolina. He grew pears, apples, peaches, and figs. We always took our walks in the backyard while chatting about life. While walking, he liked to show off his trees, but I always had questions. One morning, as we were walking, I pointed out a few trees and asked, "Which one is this? Which one is that?"

His responses were "I told you that's my peach tree" or "That's my fig tree."

My response to him was "How would I have known? There are no fruit!"

He said, "That's because, every time fruit grows on it, the deer come and eat them off the trees." Then, he said, "But I figured out something. The further away they are from the house, the more likely the trees are to lose their fruit, so I dug up the trees and planted them closer to the house, so I could keep an eye on them, and I put a hedge around them to keep away the deer."

When you're positioned closer to the *house* (to the things of God, to an assembly of believers, to people of God who have the same godly principles as you), you're in a blessed place. Staying closer to the house, to the things of God, will nurture your "fruit." It's one thing to say that you're blessed, but it's another thing to show signs of being blessed. When you are blessed and in a blessed place, you are blessed in your health; you are blessed in your wealth, and you're blessed with all that you need when you need it! God wants His children to be blessed at all times, in all seasons.

Deuteronomy 28:1-3 (NIV): If you fully obey the *Lord* your God and carefully follow all his commands, I give you today, the *Lord* your God will set you high above all the nations on earth. *All these blessings will come on you and accompany you if you obey the Lord your God: You will be blessed in the city and blessed in the country.*

A blessed place is when we take delight in the things of God. A blessed place is when we are planted and yield fruit in our due season. A blessed place is when we prosper in all that God has assigned our hands to do.

When you are in a blessed place and everything is working together for good, whatever you do is going to result in a blessed life! Live blessed, be blessed, speak blessed! You are a child of the Most High God! It's time to act like it!

Dear Father, thank you for reminding us that, when we are planted, we, too, can bear much fruit and live a blessed life. Forgive us for the times we didn't profess how blessed we really were. In Jesus' name, amen.

DAY 9

THE GOD OF TOMORROW

Matthew 6:34 (KJV): *Therefore do not worry about tomorrow, for tomorrow will worry about its own things. Sufficient for the day is its own trouble.*

D o you find yourself worrying about everything? Is your brain on a constant spin cycle, worrying about how you're going to pay a bill or bills? Do you worry about your kids? About your relationships? Your jobs? After you've finished worrying, did it make a difference? Did anything change?

The Dutch watchmaker and writer Corrie ten Boom said, "Worry does not empty tomorrow of its sorrow. It empties today of its strength. If you want to be happy, do not dwell in the past, do not worry about the future, focus on living fully in the present. Instead of worrying about what you cannot control, shift your energy to what you can create."

Your body responds to worry. It can start to have a toxic effect on the glands, the nervous system, and the heart, eventually leading to heart attacks, increased risk of strokes, and stomach ulcers.

With excessive worry, your immune system has little time to recover, so you become even more tired and lethargic. Worrying, also, has an effect on your brain. Excessive worry disturbs your peace of mind; it's harder for you to concentrate on one task at a time. Worry makes it difficult for you to fall asleep at night. Now you're suffering from insomnia, and you start to worry about that!

But another translation says it this way: Give your entire attention to what God is doing right now, and don't get worked up about what may or may not happen tomorrow. God will help you deal with whatever hard things come up when the time comes (The Message Bible). But we find ourselves worrying about things, even though things corrode, dry, rot, lose value, get lost, or become unnecessary. Things are not God. Things are not relationships. Things are not who you are but that which God allows you to have as a result of seeking Him! There are those within the body of Christ who have made things a priority, instead of making God a priority.

When people of God feel out of sorts, it's because attaining more things has taken precedence over a relationship with God. As a result, we are not a threat to the kingdom of darkness. Things ought not to be the focus but rather relationships, so the kingdom can be advanced. These things… we think we need them. We desire them because they make us look better, feel better, live better, have more to talk about, or more to boast about. These things become the very focal point of our existence. But when things are not the focus, a true relationship takes place. There is something about resting in God, whether we know what tomorrow will bring or not. When we rest in God, we are fully putting our faith in Him. Whatever tomorrow brings, it is what it is. Faith is the bridge that helps us cross over from today into tomorrow. Hebrews 11:1 says: Now faith is. Faith is present. Faith is needed the moment you need it.

In this text, God reminds us that He sees your tomorrow while He blesses you in your today. I find this text to be necessary for the people of God because many have faith in God, as long as it's today. As long as it's today, my yoke is easy, and my burden is light. As long as it's today, I can do all things through Christ. Today, I can see, feel, hear, understand, be in, yet recollect what I did yesterday. Today, a glimpse of time. Today, this present moment. And so, we believe we don't need help with our today. We can handle today. We can envision today. We can call forth today because we're in it. We can stand in faith today, in the present. The unfortunate thing about God's people is that we choose to have control in everything we do. And so, as long as we can exist in our "today" while controlling our tomorrows, we will always try to be one step ahead of God. God is in full control of everything! He's omniscient. We've got to deal with this enemy called "tomorrow" because it has a hold on what God is doing in our lives today. Tomorrow is the enemy of God's people. As long as the enemy can keep our focus on tomorrow, we will always fail to be in the present. Even with the very simplicities of life, we find ourselves inquiring about or discussing them. What's the weather going to be like... tomorrow? What am I going to wear... tomorrow? What should I cook for dinner... tomorrow? I've got to be at work earlier... tomorrow. That bill is due...tomorrow.

When this is our norm, it produces an anxiety-driven believer, who constantly worries about tomorrow and is never in the moment. Therefore, as long as your focus is always on tomorrow, you will miss whatever God desires to do in your today because you have already created an agenda for tomorrow. That's why the text says: Don't worry what may or may not happen in tomorrow. Today is important to God. We know that because He gives us this model prayer early in the chapter to teach us how to pray. In verse 11, it says: Give us this day. When you are praying about this day, it automatically removes you from the cares of tomorrow and the complaints of yesterday!

Deal with today and make room for God to deal with tomorrow. Somehow, there is a need to control something, and as long as today has already started and happened, we want to get tomorrow started, so we can orchestrate and control that. And so God is saying to us, "Let me, who created today, take care of your tomorrows. Allow me, who knows what your tomorrow will hold, take care of your tomorrows. Allow me, who loves you so much, to step into your tomorrows. Allow me, who is the keeper of tomorrow, to cascade over your mind and over your thoughts and bring calm to your tomorrow."

He is the God of tomorrow, yet, somehow, we cast Him aside and attempt to deal with our tomorrows on our own, even though the text says: Don't worry about tomorrow. God will help you deal with it when the time comes. He's concerned about what concerns us, and if we can just praise Him in and for today, then whatever may come, He still deserves the glory. The hymn says: "Whatever my lot, thou has taught me to say it is well!" The text answers the question, Why don't I need to worry about tomorrow? Simply because God will always provide.

Most often, worry is centered around provision. Will I have enough? Where is it going to come from? God is Jehovah Jireh, the God who provides. His provision is not based on what we need, but who He is! He is Provision. God wants to add to your life. When you just allow God to be God, He will add to your life. Anything or anyone that does not add to your life is taking away from your life. John 10:10 (KJV) says: The thief cometh not but for to steal kill and destroy, but I've come that you might have life and have it to the full. The enemy steals; God adds. Stay in the present. Let God be the God of your tomorrow. He has so much in store for your life.

Dear Father, when we find ourselves worrying about things that are out of our control, teach us to rest in you, knowing that you do all things well and with us in mind. Amen.

DAY 10

WHEN GOD REMOVES YOUR EXCUSES

John 5:1-9 (KJV): *After this there was a feast of the Jews, and Jesus went up to Jerusalem.* ² *Now there is in Jerusalem by the Sheep Gate a pool, which is called in Hebrew, Bethesda,*[a] *having five porches.* ³ *In these lay a great multitude of sick people, blind, lame, paralyzed, waiting for the moving of the water.* ⁴ *For an angel went down at a certain time into the pool and stirred up the water; then whoever stepped in first, after the stirring of the water, was made well of whatever disease he had.*[b] ⁵ *Now a certain man was there who had an infirmity thirty-eight years.* ⁶ *When Jesus saw him lying there, and knew that he already had been in that condition a long time, He said to him, 'Do you want to be made well?'* ⁷ *The sick man answered Him, 'Sir, I have no man to put me into the pool when the water is stirred up; but while I am coming, another steps down before me.' Jesus said to him, 'Rise, take up your bed and walk.'* ⁹ *And immediately the man was made well, took up his bed, and walked. And that day was the Sabbath.*

I read a quote recently that said: "If it's important to you, you'll find a way; if it's not, you'll find an excuse." Excuses, in many cases, are our politically correct way of responding to things we don't want to do or believe we can't do. Oftentimes, excuses can be used for so long that we begin to believe them ourselves. You know the kind of excuse that says, "I would save more money, but I've got so many bills" or "I would eat better, but I work late, so I grab whatever I can get on the way home."

In this text, Jesus asked the man one critical question in order to get one critical answer, and that question was,

"Do you want to get well?" He had become a product of his environment, so he came up with an excuse that worked for him and that he'd begun to believe.

"I've got nobody to put me in the pool," he said.

Have you ever made an excuse for yourself for so long that it just began to work for you, so much so that others affirmed your excuse? What do you do when God removes your excuse(s)? What do you do when God removes every possibility that you can come up with and says, "Ok, we've got that out of the way, now what? What's your excuse now?" You said you'd love to give more to the church or to organizations that help those in need when you got your hands on a couple of extra dollars, but the moment you got some extra money, you decided to treat yourself to a spa day, a great meal at your favorite restaurant, or a quick trip to your favorite place; in other words, it never got done. Excuses! What God shows us in this text is excuses must be received for them to be valid! In other words, I have to get somebody to come in agreement with my situation, thereby making my situation or condition, in this case, an actual problem. Look at the text! Here comes the excuse!

The man said, "I have no one to put me in the pool!"

Jesus said, "Get up. Take up your mat and walk."

Jesus didn't come into agreement with his condition. In other words, he didn't entertain that conversation. He didn't say, "How come nobody put you in the pool?" He didn't say, "Didn't they know you couldn't walk?" He merely said, "Get up. Take up your mat and walk!" You see, it's easy to jump on the bandwagon of excuses, rather than being a participant in the promise. The truth of the matter is, anyone that was around the pool with him could have gotten him to the pool. Even if you are blind, you can walk! Even if you're sick, you can push somebody to the pool. What's been happening at the pool (in our churches, on our jobs, in our families, or other places of influence) is that we are all coming in agreement with what we see, rather than the potential of what can be! God has equipped us!

You are a child of God! You have God in you. You have the ability to stand on God's Word and believe! But as soon as somebody needs a problem solved, you direct them to somebody else! Excuses! Or as soon as you come into a problem yourself, your faith goes out the window, and you come up with an excuse: "I have no one to put me in the pool." How much longer shall we blame others for things that we are equipped to do, had we just believed?

Jesus is showing us, in this text, that we are equipped to make a difference in the lives of those who are sick, lame, and afflicted. This text is the manifestation of the greater works that Jesus speaks of in John 14:12 (NIV): Very truly I tell you, whoever believes in me will do the works I have been doing, and they will do even greater things than these, because I am going to the Father. God has equipped us to speak to a thing and it be done in Jesus's name. Mark 11:23 (KJV) says: "For verily I say unto you, that whosoever shall say unto this mountain, be thou removed, and be thou cast into the sea; and shall not doubt in his heart but shall believe that those things which he saith shall come to pass; he shall have whatsoever he saith." No more excuses. Trust in God. Trust in His Word.

Dear Father, thank you for making a way for us during our difficult times. Forgive us for making excuses and for casting blame

on others when you have enabled us to stand firmly on your Word.
In Jesus' name, Amen.

MOM'S MEMOS

DO YOU KNOW THE AUTHOR?

A friend told me she had just read the most uninteresting book of her life. As time went on, she became engaged to a young man. One night, she said to him, "I have a book in my library, and the author's initials are the same as yours. Isn't that a coincidence?"

"I don't think so," he said.

"Why not?"

"For the simple reason, I wrote the book."

That night, she sat up all night, reading the book again. This time, it seemed to be the most interesting story she had ever read. The once-dull book was fascinating because now she knew and loved the author. So, it is with a child of God. He or she knows and loves the author; therefore, the book is read with a different attitude and understanding. Do you know the author?

DAY 11

I HOPE YOUR LIGHTS DON'T GO OUT

Matthew 5:16 (KJV): *Let your light so shine before men, that they may see your good works, and glorify your Father which is in heaven.*

The year was 2012. The mayor of Richmond, Virginia declared a state of emergency because, within twenty-four hours, we were about to be hit by Hurricane Sandy.

The news journalist said this event would be, not only catastrophic, but historic. There had never be a storm equivalent to what was about to take place. People were in every store throughout the city, buying D-cell batteries, flashlights, and bread and peanut butter. Bottled water was flying off the shelves. Candles were being sold like never before. Generators and wood were being sought after at every outlet. The amazing thing was, people were buying all these items at any price. As I observed the frenzy, I noticed that, among every ethnicity, nationality, age, and gender, people were talking to one another. In many cases, strangers were speaking to people who, under any other circumstance, they would not speak to. The following words permeated the aisles of stores across the city: "I hope your lights don't go out." My ears were attuned to these conversations because this was going to be an unprecedented event, according to weather history.

Fear loomed throughout the city. However, if there had ever been a state of emergency announced, it should have been the moment you chose to not follow God! That's an emergency.

Storms come. Devastation will occur within all of our lives. We just have got to be prepared! Storms are a part of life. Storms are inevitable. God's people blame the enemy for storms, rather than understanding the fact that storms will undeniably be a part of every believer's life! People are more concerned about the consequences of a storm than they are about the consequences of not following the God of the storm. We are more concerned about the possible inconveniences of losing the Internet, television, and telephones, than we are about believing in the God of the universe. We are more concerned about our food going bad in the refrigerator than we are about the creator of all vegetation. Now, I'm not suggesting that we don't use wisdom during times such as these, but we must understand that God has got this all under control. He is a strategic God, not a haphazard God. I heard a pastor say, "God doesn't make mistakes. God makes decisions." What He does is intentional, not happenstance, but something happens to people when the reality of devastation seems like it's coming closer and closer to their door. Something happens to people's thought processes when the reality of being in darkness becomes more and more inevitable.

Therefore, I came to the conclusion that mayhem finds itself in stores across the region when a state of emergency is declared because people are afraid of what the darkness will bring. I asked myself, "What is it about darkness in the natural that does not transfer to darkness in the spiritual? Why are people content with their lives being in darkness in the spiritual but will go to extremes to create light in the natural? What are we, as believers,

NOT showing in the spiritual that is not causing the same amount of doggedness when it comes to the reasons why we ought not want to stay in darkness?"

Truth be told, people are really afraid of the dark. There is a sense of helplessness in the dark, so people of God ought to exude light. In order to understand the fullness of light in the spiritual, we must understand it in the natural.

The first principle of light is that light moves faster than sound. Many of today's saints have a lot to say. We are talking Christians, but we are not all walking Christians, meaning we talk about God but do no exhibit any fruit! Galatians 5:22 (NIV) says: But the fruit of the Spirit is love, joy, peace, forbearance, kindness, goodness, faithfulness. Light must be seen with the eyes and not with the ears. So, if we are light, then we must strive to allow our light to be seen and not heard.

There's a story of a man who went out to sea to fish in the middle of the winter. He enjoyed fishing because that was his time to be with the Lord, but this certain man hadn't prepared for the storm. He realized he didn't have a shortwave radio, a survival kit, extra rope... nothing. All he had was a small bag of food and some water. As the storm grew closer, his goal was to try to get to the other side, but he struggled as he tried to steer the boat to the other side; the winds, however, overtook him and caused him to go out further into the deep. It was dark. It was cold, and it was frightening. He began hearing the voice of help in the distance. He heard the voice say, "We're here to help you. Just be calm!"

Sadly, the closer he thought he was getting to the voice, the further away he actually was from it.

Another voice said, "Steer in the direction of my voice."

He was getting discouraged because he wasn't getting any closer at all. Hours passed. As night fall was at its peak, the temperatures dropped even more. With trembling hands, he managed to break a piece of seashell that had come in the net while fishing and scratched out these words on the walls of his boat: Heard voice. Couldn't see your light. The man eventually died at sea.

This sad commentary is synonymous with many believers. People are dying, having not seen our light, because we're so busy talking about our God, but not showing our God. People are in the middle of their storms, looking for our light, while we're busy calling out to them and talking to them, trying to help, moving people in the direction of our voice, instead of moving them in the direction of our light! Light moves faster than sound! Your light will get there before your mouth does! It's time for the people of God to be light. God is calling us to deeper things. God is calling us out of some things. God is calling His people to elevate minds and encourage hearts.

I speak to your light. There are some needed changes in the lives of God's people so that the unchurched, non-believers, non-conference goers, non-Bible toters, the people that don't speak in tongues, and those that don't know the hymns can come to know Him because of our light and not because of our speaking. God is calling us to shine some light in the dark places! People are concerned about their dark places. The safety of their children - dark places. Their health - dark places. Their money - dark places. Their relationships - dark places. Their homes - dark places. Their jobs - dark places. God is calling us to the dark places. I hope your lights don't go out because they're needed in the dark places. God is calling us to be light, so be light!

Dear Father, there are many that are searching for our light as they go through their dark moments in life. Shine through us and tug on our hearts when we find ourselves talking too much. Amen.

DAY 12

BE A CONQUEROR

Romans 8:37 (KJV): *Nay in all these things we are more than conquerors through him that loved us.*

Some time ago, I read a book where the author not only disclosed the deepest details of her cancer journey, but she, also, said that she was not just a cancer survivor but a conqueror. I thought that was such a profound statement. It's a blessing to be a survivor, but it speaks even more to the character of someone who chooses to be a conqueror.

The text says: In all things we are more than conquerors. Being "more than" means you have God's strength and love within you. However, some of us are going to just be survivors. Survivors of diseases. Survivors of dysfunctional families. Survivors of bankruptcy. Survivors of divorce. We can always take it a step further and understand that anybody can survive, but not everybody can conquer.

A survivor gets through a situation and is just happy to have gotten through to the other side. A survivor might get through cancer but then can't get through bankruptcy. A survivor can get through a situation and then has to talk about it on the other side. A survivor reminds other people that they are surviving. A survivor, oftentimes, will not always come out better but might be bitter on the other side. A survivor doesn't always have gratitude in their vocabulary but one of entitlement and relief.

It takes the strength of God to conquer. It takes the tenacity of God to conquer. It takes faith in God to conquer. It takes trust in God to conquer. It takes hope in God to conquer. A conqueror says, "No matter what, God is on my side." A conqueror says, "Nothing is going to separate me from the love of Christ."

When you are a conqueror, there's nothing too hard for God. When you are a conqueror, things will come up that are out of your control, yet you understand that God is in control and still on your side. When you are a conqueror, how you begin to see and say things changes. Once you learn how to conquer, then no matter what comes your way, you're still a conqueror! Some of us need to first conquer ourselves. That which requires conquering usually begins with us. If you don't conquer self, you will be defeated by self! Your language needs to change about you. Your vision needs to change about you. Your hearing needs to change about you. At some point, you just need to affirm yourself, "I am more than a conqueror. I am the head and not the tail. I am fearfully and wonderfully made. I am the beloved of Christ."

You just need to conquer yourself!

This is the same chapter that talks about carnality. This is the same chapter that talks about walking after the things of the Spirit. This is the same chapter that talks about anything that goes against the knowledge of God. This is the same chapter that talks about the Spirit bearing witness with our own spirit. This is the same chapter that talks about suffering in this present time. It talks about being delivered from the bondage of corruption. It talks about all things working together for good. It talks about being conformed to the image of the son. This chapter reminds us that we are God's elect! How, then, do we reconcile calling ourselves "survivors" and not "conquers"? God is our redeemer! God is our protector!

God is our provider! This same God can do all things but fail! And if you're going to be a conqueror, then you must first identify what you're conquering. Anything that needs conquering is anything that comes to separate us from our faith in God. Conquer it. You can't conquer what you don't identify. That's why the Bible says: He conquered death, hell, and the grave. He didn't just survive death on Calvary's cross; He conquered it! He has called us to be conquerors, not survivors! And once you've conquered a thing, don't look back. Press toward the prize of the high calling in Christ Jesus. Move forward in the things of God, then make a decision to be a conqueror.

Dear Father, when things come up in our lives that are out of our control, help us to remember that we are more than conquerors and not just survivors because you have all things in control. Amen.

DAY 13

THE CHOICE IS YOURS

Joshua 24:14-15 (KJV): *Now therefore fear the LORD and serve him in sincerity and in truth: and put away the gods which your fathers served on the other side of the flood, and in Egypt; and serve ye the LORD.* *15 And if it seem evil unto you to serve the LORD, choose you this day whom ye will serve; whether the gods which your fathers served that were on the other side of the flood, or the gods of the Amorites, in whose land ye dwell: but as for me and my house, we will serve the LORD.*

Back in the day, Black Sheep, a rap duo from Queens, New York, recorded a song called "The Choice is Yours." It was very popular. The lyrics went, Who's the black sheep? What's the black sheep? The hook said: You can get with this, or you can get with that... You can get with this, or you can get with that...I think you'll get with this 'cause this is where it's at. In essence, you have a choice, but the choice is ultimately yours.

There are many things in the world that capture our attention on a daily basis, causing us to have to make choices. The problem is, we have too many options. For the believer who is adamant about doing the will of God, those choices should not be hard to make at all. But the believer who is straddling the fence from week to week will find themselves in positions of chaos, unproductivity, and frustration, as they watch the consequences of their choices being played out. You can get with this, or you can get with that. The choice is yours!

As I get older and become more in tune with my relationship in Christ Jesus, I've made some very important decisions, including I will no longer speak the way I've spoken, act the way I've acted, or even live the way I've lived! Although it has not been easy, I made these choices. The problem is we don't always like to make choices or decisions, so we play it safe and straddle the line. What do we know about choices? Choices are only difficult to make when something else appears to be better. There will be moments in our lives when we have to make a choice. The problems ensue when we have other options. On our spiritual journey, the enemy depends on the indecisive believer. As it is in the natural, so it is in the spiritual.

For example, I don't like to go grocery shopping because there are so many choices. You just can't buy one box of cereal; now you have a choice of forty different brands! I find myself knowing exactly what I need, but by the time I get inside, there are too many options to choose from, so what happens is, I purchase something that I don't need because I became distracted given the many options and made some wrong choices based upon one moment in time. Some of these big box stores depend on the impulsivity and indecisiveness of shoppers, so they set up a table that allows customers to sample something that wasn't even on their shopping list or on their minds to get. After they've sampled it, the first thing they say is, "I've got to have this." Then the customers ask, "Where do I find this in the store?"

In most cases, because they don't want the customers to go too far from the sample table, for fear of them changing their minds, their responses might be, "We have some right here. How many do you want?"

The body of Christ needs to take the example of some of these big box stores. There are people that don't always know what they need, so we need to be prepared with a sample. A sample of our testimony! A sample of how God has brought us from a mighty long way! A sample of how He delivered us and set us free! A sample of God's love! A sample of God's healing power! A sample of His light!

If there's no foundation, you might choose the wrong thing at the wrong time. If there is no relationship with God, you make choices based on impulsivity, immediacy, or fatigue. In other words, you might not be tired in the physical sense, but you could be tired of stuff in your life, so you make any choice, but choices have consequences. But the time has come, and is yet coming, that those choices that we have made without the discernment of and guidance from the Holy Spirit will have an adverse effect on our now. The text says: Put away the gods. Put away the distractions. Put away those things that keep you from serving Him. Put away those things that keep Him at arm's distance from you. Put away those people that hinder you and keep you from His will. Make a choice! Jesus, the Son of the living God, made a choice. He said, not my will, but "thy will be done," and He gave up His life for our sins on the cross of Calvary. In other words, at some point, we have to make a choice, even unto death. It's time for us to make a choice! Choose ye this day whom you will serve. You can get with this, or you can get with that. The choice is yours.

Dear Father, when there are so many choices to make, through the power of Holy Spirit, enable us to hear your voice and make the right decisions for our lives. In Jesus' name, Amen.

DAY 14

THE GOSPEL ACCORDING TO THE OLYMPICS

Hebrews 12:1 (KJV): *¹Wherefore seeing we also are compassed about with so great a cloud of witnesses, let us lay aside every weight, and the sin which doth so easily beset us, and let us run with patience the race that is set before us. Looking unto Jesus the author and finisher of our faith; who for the joy that was set before him endured the cross, despising the shame, and is set down at the right hand of the throne of God.*

Many people are fond of the Olympics and, in most cases, have a favorite event. In most of these events, be it swimming, gymnastics, or track and field, there's always a crowd. In the crowd are the mommas, the daddies, the coaches, and other family members and friends. Also, in that same crowd, is the competition! One thing you learn as a competitor is that there will always be people in the crowd yelling at and saying something negative to you, but you find out, early on in your training, that you can't listen to everybody's voice because everybody isn't in your corner. Everybody isn't a part of your team. My question to you is, who is in your ear, and what are you listening to? The Bible says: My sheep know my voice and a stranger they will not follow (John 10:4-5).

Retired Olympic gymnast Dominique Dawes, in an interview that led up to the 2012 Olympics, said that she walked around the arena, praying for and cheering on Gabby Douglas. But in as much as she cheered, cried, hollered, and prayed, she wasn't her coach, so Gabby had no reason to look at her for pointers or confirmation. Likewise, there are people in our lives that are calling out to us, cheering us on, and giving us life pointers, but they are not who we should be looking to for confirmation. Our ears should be listening for His voice.

Usain Bolt, a retired Jamaican sprinter and Olympic record holder, in an interview after his race, said, "I've learned, over the years, that if you start thinking about the race, it stresses you out a little bit. I just try to relax and think about what I'm going to do after the race."

We can learn from these Olympians. As we go through our lives, each of us have our own races to run. Each of us have our own destinations. However, we cannot allow the weight of life to burden us to the point where nothing gets accomplished, where we can't finish the race. When we carry the weight around with us, it makes getting to our destinations even more burdensome. The scripture says: Lay aside every weight that so easily beset you. There are some things that God has in store for you, and while you are trying to hold on to that thing or that weight, your race is being held up! You can't get to the end of where God has for you while you're holding on to the entangled things.

Some time ago, I had a beautiful delicate gold chain, but it had a tangle in it, and the tangles were in a clump in one specific place on the chain. I had to get somewhere the morning I decided to wear this chain, so tussling with the tangle was holding me up. After some time, I decided that I would rotate the tangle to the back of my neck where no one could see it. When I arrived at my destination, I was immediately complimented on my beautiful delicate chain, but what the person didn't see was the tangle that I had strategically shifted.

What do you do when you're trying to show up in life, looking perfectly put together, knowing you are hiding your entanglements? Of course, we only want to show our good parts, but what we don't consider are those who are behind us. Our spouses are behind us. Our children and grandchildren are behind us. Our nieces and nephews are behind us. At least, if we're going to show up, we ought to be transparent about our entanglements, so we can help those who are watching us from behind.

The text says: Let us run the race with patience that is set before you. We all have our own races to run. The problem is many of us are tired before we even start the race. The Olympians each had to go through preliminaries. These were the qualifying races before the real race. The competition before the competition. The preliminaries qualify you based on your time. To think of anything requires you to think of it within the context of time. The right thing at the wrong time is the wrong thing. Timing is everything. Although this phrase is quite common, there is a great deal of truth in it. The difference between Gabby Douglas, Simone Biles, and their competition was timing. The difference came in what they did while they were in the middle of their competition. In the Olympics, the difference between those that compete and those that make it to the end is all in their timing!

What God has in store for His people is predicated upon two things — your obedience to His voice and your obedience to His timing. If you can hear His voice today and decide to move upon what you've heard three months from now, your timing is off, and because He's God, the anointing doesn't have to be upon you to do that thing at that time. You may have missed your time.

Many of us on our life journey get tired at the preliminaries. Many of us celebrate ourselves in the preliminaries and are content with not going any further. We have these proverbial "I made it over" parties, as if we've done something spectacular and phenomenal, but really, we haven't made it over, we've just made it to!

If you go back and reread the Olympians interviews, what you'll hear them saying is "I beat my time from the preliminaries" because what's behind you is the preliminaries, the past. You don't need to celebrate the past. That's over. Celebrate now. Celebrate the fact that you have gotten beyond that and are now looking at this. That is a testimony in itself!

Finally, the text says: Looking unto Jesus, the author and finisher of our faith. In this season, you must stay focused. The common theme for every Olympian was their ability to stay focused. Some had lost some coaches or family members and weren't told until after they had won their medals. Others had done nothing else but stayed in the race until that day came.

We must stay focused. The text says: Look to Jesus. There will be many things that come our way that may cause us to become distraught and distracted. Some of these Olympians said they did nothing but train for all the years that led up to their competitions. They watched no TV, and their social lives were limited to nothing but that which was needed for their victories. When you get to the place where God is your focus and nothing else is relative to you but victory, then you will understand the life of an Olympian, but more importantly, you will understand the life of a child of God!

Gabby, Simone, and Usain each had their focuses. No matter what was going on in the stands, they were focused on their victories. There are times when you've got to do what you've got to do to gain the victory. The enemy is betting on you to lose your focus, go back to your old self, and not fight this good fight of faith. He's depending on you to celebrate at the preliminaries. He's depending on you to miss your timing! He's depending on you to not desire the taste of victory but to be complacent with your certificate of participation! What the enemy doesn't know is that you will continue to press toward the prize of the high calling in Christ Jesus. What the enemy doesn't know is that the favor of God is upon your life. What the enemy doesn't know is that you plan on seeking the kingdom of God and His righteousness. You are focused, and I declare and decree, on this day, you are closer to the finish line than you think and victory is in your view.

Dear Father, thank you for helping us to run our race with patience, but when we become distracted by the voices of others, remind us that we can be more victorious when our eyes are upon you, as we remain in your timing. Amen.

DAY 15

WHERE'S GRACE?

Ephesians 4:7 (KJV): *But unto every one of us is given grace according to the measure of the gift of Christ.*

Where's grace? Grace is missing! Grace is not a person in this case. Grace is the love of God shown to the loveless. Grace is the peace of God shown to the restless. Grace is love extended toward a person who doesn't deserve it. God's grace is His unmerited favor. We should live every day by God's grace, but grace is missing from the lives of believers. Grace is missing from the church.

It's amazing to me that there are those within the body of Christ who desire for grace to be extended to them when they have gone astray but cannot extend an ounce of grace to someone else when they have fallen short. Romans 3:23 (NIV): For all have sinned and fall short of the glory of God. It's even more amazing to me how we can take tally marks of the sins of others and have episodic amnesia when it comes to the things that we do. God seeks men and women after His own heart. God created us, so he knows our strengths and our weaknesses. He knows our thoughts and our ways.

There are many within the church who are apostolic bullies. They are bullying people into acting like, being like, thinking like us, particularly, as long as we're in the church. They never extend grace but are always sitting anxiously in the seat of judgment. Whenever someone disagrees with them, their theologies, or their doctrines, they quickly dismiss them and cut them off. Sometimes, they even go further and call them "the enemy" or "the devil." Where's grace? People are taking a stand, but that stand isn't always kind. It isn't always loving. It isn't always timely, and it definitely isn't always God.

Yes! We've got to stand up for something in the kingdom of God, but before you take a stand for something, why not stand for what God stands for? Why can't we propose in our hearts to speak the good news of Jesus Christ and demonstrate love for all of God's people? Why can't we love them, even knowing what you know? Love them, in spite of themselves. Love them because God loves them.

In the late eighties, there was a book series called Where's Waldo?. Waldo was always on a journey on every page in every book. What made this colorful book so unique was that Waldo was always hidden among this chaos and confusion, and the object of the book was to find Waldo. He was never in the same place twice. But one thing about Waldo was, you knew what he was supposed to look like because he would have on the same thing and look the same way on every page. As you move through the book successfully, he becomes easier to find because you know what you are looking for. You recognize his characteristics. You could easily pick him out among all the other characters.

There are those that God has placed you among who will always seem to attract or cause chaos and confusion in their lives and in the lives of those they're around. But you have to remain constant and never changing, always extending grace, no matter what. You, the believer, must remain the same so that people can find you, and when they find you, you can lead them to the Christ. Many are looking for someone to show them grace. It is always possible to extend more grace, so God's love can be made manifest in the lives of those that need to know Him, for those that need to find Him.

There are millennials and GenXers who are waiting on the church to respond to the things of this world with grace, to the things that they contend with on a daily basis with grace, to the issues that concern them with grace. The scriptures remind us in Luke 5:31 (KJV): They that are whole need not a physician, but they that are sick. There are those crying out in their own way, but the body of Christ cannot hear the cries of the people because we are too busy taking praise breaks and "touching our neighbors" and "high-fiving" that we fail to see the tears and the hurt of the onlookers.

Grace is needed beyond Sunday, not just for Sunday. Grace is needed in the lives of people. Grace is needed because everyone isn't going to land in our churches, but they will need to experience the love of God, through God's people. How effective can we be as a body of believers if we would consider responding from grace first, before we respond with judgement and opinion? If we just let grace lead, then everything else will follow. Grace loves the unlovable. Grace is the peace of God shown to the restless. Where is grace?

Recently, I heard a pastor say, "The largest church in America is the church called 'I used to go.'" Perhaps seats would be packed in the churches across America if we would just show more grace. If His grace is sufficient for us, then we should, likewise, extend grace to others. Where's grace when you need it?

Dear Father, as you send people across our path daily, who may not always act or think like we do, help us to show grace, as an

extension of our relationship with you, that we may advance the
kingdom of God. In Jesus' name. Amen.

MOM'S MEMOS

WHO'S IN CONTROL?

A young man went out on a fishing trip with his father and two friends. Within hours of their departure from the shore, a fierce storm raged. His father yelled, "Do you have on your life jacket, son?"

"Yes, Dad," he yelled.

The two friends yelled, "We're all going to die!"

"Hold on," they yelled.

With a calmness that came from deep inside, he said to his two friends, "Do not worry. Everything is under control. My father is at the helm."

When the storms of life are raging, who's in control? Do you have that kind of assurance?

DAY 16

Tracy La'Nai Clark

WHERE ARE YOU IN THE CROWD?

Mark 5:22-34 (KJV): *And, behold, there cometh one of the rulers of the synagogue, Jairus by name; and when he saw him, he fell at his feet, And besought him greatly, saying, My little daughter lieth at the point of death: I pray thee, come and lay thy hands on her, that she may be healed; and she shall live. And Jesus went with him; and much people followed him, and thronged him. And a certain woman, which had an issue of blood twelve years, 26 And had suffered many things of many physicians, and had spent all that she had, and was nothing bettered, but rather grew worse, 27 When she had heard of Jesus, came in the press behind, and touched his garment. 28 For she said, If I may touch but his clothes, I shall be whole. 29 And straightway the fountain of her blood was dried up; and she felt in her body that she was healed of that plague. 30 And Jesus, immediately knowing in himself that virtue had gone out of him, turned him about in the press, and said, Who touched my clothes? 31 And his disciples said unto him, Thou seest the multitude thronging thee, and sayest thou, Who touched me? 32 And he looked round about to see her that had done this thing. 33 But the woman fearing and trembling, knowing what was done in her, came and fell down before him, and told him all the truth. 34 And he said unto her, Daughter, thy faith hath made thee whole; go in peace, and be whole of thy plague.*

This text may be very familiar to many because it speaks to persevering through an issue. We all have issues. For some of us, our issues may be financial; for others, they may be emotional. Then, there are the psychological and relational issues. This text speaks to suffering, healing, faith, and perseverance, but if you look closely, you will see yourself somewhere within this text. There are three types of people that can be seen right here in this text — those who follow the crowd, those who are in the crowd, and those who are crowding. The text speaks to each of these distinctive positions. Perhaps, we have heard this text from the perspective of the suffering of this woman or the ostracization of this woman because of her illnesses or even the unfortunate realization that comes with spending all you have, for the sake of getting well. But seldom do we look at the most obvious within the text — the crowd. There are times when being a part of a crowd can be to your detriment.

Can you find your place in the crowd? Too often, we hear the scriptures being proclaimed, and we remove ourselves from the biblical text, saying, "Well, that was then; this is now." But somewhere, deep within the recesses of this text, lies the truth, which is the character of the crowd.

At the onset of this text, we see those who follow the crowd. Just who are these crowd followers? We've seen these types of people before. Somehow, they never have a destination. There's no desire to end up at a strategic destination because wherever they end up is okay. These people move from place to place, following others, simply because its better somewhere else. They are following the next big thing. Following anything or anybody that moves their agenda along. Following a name they can drop at another time and place.

Followers follow with no destiny or set purpose. People that have no destiny will always follow the crowd because, usually, the crowd doesn't have a destiny either. But in the eyes of onlookers, they look like they're going somewhere; they look like they're producing something.

They look like they're getting somewhere, but they are all just "following the crowd." When you follow the crowd, there is always going to be constant movement. This kind of movement is likened to a restless spirit. When that is the case, commitment becomes secondary. I'm talking about crowd followers.

Then, the text demonstrates the second kind of person, those who are in the crowd. These are the people that hide behind folks. They are spectators with no purpose, spectators with no destiny. With no desire to move forward, they're not following anyone. They make no contribution to ministry. They take up space. They have no independent thoughts or contradictory input. They go to the local churches on special days but have no real commitment to anything. They hide in plain sight, right in the crowd.

In the text, the woman was making her way to Jesus. The need for divine healing pushed her out the door. Desperation called her to her knees. She was urgently trying to get to Jesus, and as she moved through the crowd with all her might, she was blocked by those who had no desire to move forward. They were just there, in the crowd.

Have you ever just needed to get to Jesus, but you were being blocked by those who weren't as desperate as you? You knew your healing and deliverance was predicated upon your proximity to Jesus, and when you finally got to Jesus, you found that those around you had hindered your movement by not moving at all. This is the situation this woman found herself in, and truth be told, many folks in the body of Christ do it every Sunday. There are those that are desperate and are trying to get a breakthrough, and then, there are those that are just there.

And then in verse 31, the text shows us the last group of people within the crowd. This group is those that are crowding. These people in this crowd have nothing to lose. This crowd needs a breakthrough. This crowd is desperate. This crowd will let nothing interfere with their healing. This crowd will let nothing get in the way of their deliverance. This crowd will let nothing get in between them and the Savior. I'm talking about those who are crowding.

Oftentimes, our crowding is demonstrative of our faith. Our crowding is out of our desperation. Our crowding is because we lost everything we had. Our crowding is because we've done all that we could do, so this one last time, we need God to move like never before... so we're crowding Him! This type of crowding seen by this certain woman touched Jesus in such a way that it caused him to take notice.

The text reminds us that it was in the crowding that Jesus acknowledged this certain woman. She fell down before him and told him the truth. There is something about finally getting close enough to the Master Healer that enables you to tell the whole truth and to expose the deep places of your faith. It is then that you can be made whole simply because of your crowding.

Don't let anything stop you from getting to Jesus. The woman's healing came, not because she was following Jesus, not because she was just there in the crowd, but because she was crowding or pressing into Jesus! You've got to get to the place in your life where you can get Jesus's attention and crowd him by any means necessary! If you are at a critical time in your life, crowd the Redeemer with your worship, crowd Him with your praise, crowd Him with the truth. The Healer has great things in store for your life, but you've got to be committed to pressing in to Him with all your might. Don't let anything stop you from getting to Jesus!

Dear Father, when life's circumstances have isolated us, and we have exhausted all our resources, thank you for touching us with your healing power, as we press in to you, in Jesus' name, Amen.

DAY 17

THE POWER OF LOVE

I Peter 4:8 (KJV): *Above all, love each other deeply, because love covers over a multitude of sins.*

Back in 1991, R&B Grammy award-winning artist Luther Vandross released a song entitled "The Power of Love." A portion of the lyrics went like this:

> When you're close, I can feel the power.
>
> When it's love, I can always tell.
>
> Love for me is the best thing now.
>
> It's something that I know so well.
>
> You've got to believe in love.
>
> It's a feeling that's next to none.
>
> Can't stop until we are one
>
> With the power of love.
>
> Tell everyone to try.
>
> I promise you'll reach the sky.
>
> One thing that we can't deny
>
> *Is the power of love.*

This song should be our sentiment, as we seek to love one another as God desires. The foundation of the church should be based on how we *love* each other, rather than how we *judge* each other. This song speaks to the characteristics of love. *Love*, the text says, *covers a multitude of sins.* So how come there are so many *don'ts* within the various religions and denominations?

Don't date. Don't wear earrings. Don't dance. Don't eat this. Don't say that. And the list goes on and on. With all these *don'ts,* my question is, where is love in all of this? Why would people want to come to church, or even to God, if we can't show love from the very beginning? Let love win them to Christ! Let love dictate what you do! Let God's love be *at work* in your life! There are times we may not agree with things, people, or lifestyles, but love should always supersede our opinions simply because it's about God and what pleases God, not what makes us comfortable. If you can love and be consistent in your love walk, in spite of what they do, they will come to Christ, eventually.

We all have our "eventually" stories. We weren't born perfect. Someone had to share God's love with us, in order to draw us to Him. The scripture says: *If I be lifted up, I'll draw all men unto myself.* There is a hymn, written by Fanny Crosby in 1875, that reminds us of how God drew us to Him. The lyrics are simple yet so profound: *Draw me nearer, nearer blessed, Lord, to the cross where thou hast died. Draw me nearer, nearer blessed, Lord, to thy precious, bleeding side.*

Love draws. Love does not discriminate. But what would life be like if we all were not loved for one reason or another? Not loved because you're too fat, because you're too skinny, because you're too dark, because you're too light. Not loved because you're too old, because you're too young. Not loved because you're not from this country, because you're female, because you're male. Not loved because you're single, because you're married, because you're divorced. Not loved because you have special needs, because you had a child out of wedlock, because you don't have a child, because you're a foster child, because you are adopted. Can you imagine not being loved?

Let love guide your decisions. Let love be your motive. Let love be your agenda. Love will always prevail! Love someone in spite of what you know. Love, for too long, has had a contingency clause. If they, at least, do this, then I can love them. If they think this way, then I can love them. If they live this way, then I can love them. If they dress this way, then I can love them. Love should have no contingency clause. Love should just be! The scriptures tell us about the power of love in John 3:16, the ultimate picture of love: *For God so loved the world that he gave his one and only Son, that whoever believes in him shall not perish but have eternal life.*

Love exceeds (so loved)

Love includes (the world)

Love gives (that He gave)

Love sacrifices (His only Son)

Love is inclusive (whosoever believes)

Love is concerned (shall not perish but have)

Love considers your destiny (eternal life)

Let God's love rule your thoughts and actions today. God's love is the greatest love of all.

Dear Father, thank you for loving us deeply. May we show love to our brothers and sisters, despite what we know, remembering that you first loved us, all the way to the cross. In Jesus' name. Amen.

DAY 18

I'VE GOT TRUST ISSUES

Proverbs 3:5-7 (KJV): *Trust in the LORD with all thine heart; and lean not unto thine own understanding. In all thy ways acknowledge him, and he shall direct thy paths. Be not wise in thine own eyes: fear the LORD, and depart from evil.*

The foundation of all relationships has one thing in common, and that is trust. We all know someone who has dealt with trust issues. Those that work or have worked in corporate America may be familiar with the team-building games and events that are used to build trust among colleagues, in the hopes of fostering a more productive work environment. One of the games is to pair people off, have someone stand in front of you, have that person free fall backward, and you catch them. The true test of trust was not whether they were going to be caught, but the real measure of trust was whether they could look straight ahead while free falling backward. In these events, the people were paired with those whom they worked closely and directly with. They knew them. They knew their character. They understood their strengths and weaknesses. They knew their families. They would often have meals together. But something triggered when they had to stand in front of them and trust them enough to not let them fall. Often, it was at that point that the one standing in front would walk away and say, "I can't do it. I don't trust you. You might let me fall."

There are times when our responses to life's circumstances are demonstrative of our trust in God. We don't fully trust God to do what He said, so we make attempts to work things out, rather than wait on God. In other words, we walk away because He might let us fall. The scripture says: All things work together for good, but in our anxious moments, we fail to wait, showing God, that we really do have trust issues. The Oxford Dictionary defines trust as "a firm belief in the reliability, truth, ability or strength of someone or something." For example, we trust people who are benevolent toward us, who have integrity, and whose actions correspond to their words. We trust someone we can count on to consistently do what is right. Within the context of a relationship, we trust our loved ones if he or she is predictable, reliable, and honest. Then, there's trust in God. For some reason, we put that on a whole 'nother playing field. God is deeper than what we can fathom or think. The Bible says: No eye has seen, no ear has heard, no mind has conceived what God has prepared for those who love Him... but God has revealed it to us by His spirit. The spirit searches all things, even the deep things of God (1 Corinthians 2:9-10).

Although it might seem like a simple concept, you'd be surprised at how many believers don't trust God. They may love God, but they really don't trust Him. They may even believe God, but trusting Him, somehow, requires so much more than what they are willing to give up.

Trusting God requires not knowing yet still believing. Trusting God requires not understanding yet still waiting. Not walking, not running but being able to stand still and trust God. Psalm 46:10 says: Be still and know that I am God. Trusting God requires us to remove ourselves from the result. Trusting is the only verb that is opposite of its actual meaning. In other words, you have to do without doing.

Many of us believe we're trusting God, but in the back of our minds, we're trusting God based on our timeline of events. Trusting God does not require our input. Trusting God allows us to lay back in the arms of the Father, whether we know what's going to happen next or not. God desires our full trust in Him. Even when we don't see it, we can trust Him until it happens. My question to you is, do you fully trust God, even when you don't know what's going to happen next? I implore you to trust Him, even when you can't trace Him. God knows our beginning from our end. Would you rather follow what you believe is right or wait and trust God for what we know is right? God will always have our best interests in mind. His plan is to prosper us, not to harm us, to give us a hope and a future. Fall back into his arms and trust that He won't let you fall.

Dear Father, because we have trusted others who have not had our best interests at heart, we find trusting difficult. Show us how to fall into your loving arms and trust you with our whole heart as we navigate this life. Amen.

DAY 19

STRENGTH IN YOUR WEAK MOMENTS

Philippians 4:11-13 (KJV): *I can do all things through Christ which strengtheneth me.*

As believers in Jesus Christ, the Word of God is our lifeline. It is to be believed, trusted, and adhered to. However, when weak moments show their faces along our spiritual journey, worshipping God and having strong faith in the Word of God should not be the last things we engage in; instead, they should be the first things. Somehow, there is a disconnect between that which is proclaimed on Sunday and the response to life's circumstances beyond Sunday. The promises of God are "yea" and "amen," but when folks are going through their stuff, not only can they not remember His promises, but they don't utilize them as the *only* solution! When these times occur, we can trust the scripture that says: *I can do all things through Christ who strengthens me.* So that means there's going to be a time that I'm going to need to tap into the strength of God, and when that time comes, I need to remember that God is there and that God will help me. God will strengthen me. If I can do all things through Christ that strengthens me, that lets me know that there will be some weak times. I may be weak in my mind, weak in my body, or weak in my spirit. When I don't access the strength of God during my weak moments, then my weak moments can eventually become "instabilities."

Some time ago, in the news, there was a report of a stage that collapsed at a high school in Anaheim, California. There were several students on the stage, and during a production number, the front part of the stage collapsed. After further investigation of this incident, it was found that no permit had been granted for an extension of the stage, so not only did it fall at the place of the extension, but it fell primarily as a result of the weight or the pressure that was on it, all at one time. The extension that was given made more room for more people, but no thought was given to the weight or the pressure that it would have to undertake. What am I saying? There will always be more room to do more stuff, but you must take into consideration the pressure or, rather, the consequences that you will come under. Too often, we take on projects, assignments, or other people's burdens and responsibilities that God didn't orchestrate for us. Then, we become stressed under pressure. When you come under pressure, you don't need an extension, you need something solid to hold you up! You will need a firm foundation. The Word of God is that foundation for your life's pressures, for those weak places.

One thing you must realize during your weak moments is that you are still in God's hands. No matter what it looks like. No matter how *not* like Him we may be sometimes. No matter how unloving we may present ourselves to be, we are still in God's hands. God has chosen us for His purpose. He molds us, shapes us, and reshapes us to suit Him and His plan for our lives! No matter what, we're still children of God, even during our weakest moments. Just like a potter, as he is molding, when what he forms becomes weak, or marred, he shapes it again, yet all the while remaining on the potter's wheel. Even in our weak moments, God still desires to use us.

The scriptures tell us, in Jeremiah 18:4: *But the pot he was shaping from the clay was marred in his hands.* In other words, it was impaired, bruised, hurt, tainted, or scarred, but still in His hands! Marred but you have potential! Marred but He has great things in store for you! Marred but there is a ministry in you! Marred but somebody must hear your story! Marred but you have weak moments. God is still your strength in your times of distress. Won't you let God in today? He will give you strength in your weak moments. God never fails. The scripture says: *It is in Him we live and move and have our being.* There is nothing too hard for the Lord. When we give Him our weaknesses, He has all the power to strengthen us with His might on our inner being. Let God strengthen you today.

Dear Father, in our weak moments, we depend on your strength. Keep us in your hands, always shaping us to what your perfect will and plan is for our lives. We give you thanks in advance, as you perfect us daily for your glory. In Jesus' name, Amen.

DAY 20

USE WORDS WISELY

Luke 6:45 (KJV): *A good man out of the good treasure of his heart bringeth forth that which is good; and an evil man out of the evil treasure of his heart bringeth forth that which is evil: for of the abundance of the heart his mouth speaketh.*

A Chinese proverb states: "If you wish to know the mind of a man, listen to his words." In late October of 2018, Megyn Kelly, a journalist, political commentator, and television host, made some controversial comments about blackface. The consequences of these comments resulted in her viewership plummeting and, eventually, her show being canceled.

There are words that are said in private, and there are words that are said in public. At some point, the private words will be revealed in public places. This text reminds us that what's in you will come out. That's why, every now and then, you've got to do a heart check. What's in you that does not glorify God? What's coming out of your mouth that shows the world that which you have been pondering in your heart?

Some time ago, I visited a young man in jail. His words have stuck with me to this day. He said, "Although I'm in prison, I am still free. I won't get comfortable where I am. I'm free in my mind, my spirit, my soul, so I'm only a prisoner because of where I am, but I am not a prisoner within myself. If I got out today and had a heart attack, I was never a prisoner. I was free."

Matthew 12:36 (MSG) says: There will be a time of reckoning. Words are powerful; take them seriously. Words can be your salvation. Words can also be your damnation. Think of the things that you may have said. Did it glorify God? Did it edify his people? Did it build someone up or tear someone down? Our testimonies must be full and rich, filled with God's promises. Use your words wisely. Speak boldly of what He has done in your life. Let it be known that you walk in dominion and authority, that your life is characterized by faith in Christ Jesus. The blessings of the Lord are making you rich, and you're living daily with his benefits. Speak it.

When you use your words wisely, you maximize your potential, and you are moving toward your destiny. When you use your words wisely, you can walk in divine healing, and sickness and disease will be far from you. When you use your words wisely, you can speak life and blessings over your children, over your family, and over all your affairs. We are children of the Sovereign God! He has a plan and purpose for your life. When we say what He says, God is pleased with the words we speak to ourselves and to one another.

Dear Father, forgive us when our words have caused someone to feel discouraged, unloved, or unappreciated. Show us that our words can create life and edify when used the way you have ordained. In Jesus' name, Amen.

MOM'S MEMOS

GOING THROUGH THE STORM

In September 2003, the Eastern Seaboard experienced one of the worst hurricanes in US history. The wind was fierce. The rain pounded. By eleven o'clock that morning on the day the hurricane hit, we had no lights in Raleigh, North Carolina. My husband and I could do nothing but watch from the front to the back of the house. Around three o'clock in the afternoon, we decided we would take a nap, for there was nothing else left to do. God gave us such peace in the midst of the storm that we slept like babies. And when we woke up, the storm had passed. There will be those quick, unavoidable storms that come up in our lives, but He is right in the midst, and if you trust Him, He will give you a peace that will enable you to stand any storm.

DAY 21

TURN THE LIGHT ON

Ephesians 5:8 (KJV): *For ye were sometimes darkness, but now are ye light in the LORD: walk as children of light.*

No one wants to be in the dark, but it's amazing what we can get used to. Some time ago, the lights in my stairwell went out. As a matter of fact, they had been out for quite a while. I had learned my house well enough to be able to walk around in the dark. I knew where every corner was, every piece of furniture, and every room. At night, from one level to the next level, there was nothing but darkness, and every now and then, I would stub my toe on a corner, but I knew my way around in the dark. If I could get to the top of the stairs and make it to my room that had the light, I knew I'd be fine. At the onset of my light going out in the stairwell, I used to have to hold on to the rail in order to go up the stairs. As time went on, I would count the stairs until I got to the landing. I had a system. Sometimes, I would take my cell phone with me upstairs, and that became a source of light but only when I remembered it or didn't have my hands full. There were times that I had to carry a laundry basket upstairs or other heavy items at night. What am I saying?

If you walk in darkness long enough, you begin to accommodate your situation to meet your need. There may be those in your life that have learned their way around in darkness, so much so, that they have even learned how to carry their heaviness in the dark. They have found out how to lean and depend on people and things to get them through their dark times. They have learned how not to stumble on the unexpected corners that life sends their way because they know their way around in darkness. It's not an ideal situation, but they've mastered darkness.

Most of the time, when people see them, they never see them stumbling because they have learned their way around in darkness. They never see them stumbling in their relationships or stumbling over identity issues. Never see them stumbling over old mindsets. Stumbling over bad decisions. Stumbling through life! They seem to be masters of their own fate.

In my home, I had gotten used to the darkness because the height of the ceiling in my home prevented me from replacing the broken bulbs. I didn't have access to a ladder the height of the ceiling, so I got used to the darkness. It wasn't until I got tired of feeling my way around that I called someone for help. At some point, you will get sick and tired of walking through life in the dark, and you just have to call somebody for help. When help came, I knew my problems were about to be over. It took the handyman less than two minutes to get to the top of the stairs, open his ladder, dismantle the fixture, and replace the broken bulbs. After he dismounted the ladder, he looked at me in a very puzzled manner. His eyes were squinted, as if pondering the solution to world peace, and with his head tilted, he said, "You're all set, but I have one question. How long has this light been out?"

I looked at him, scratched my head, and ashamedly said, "A long time. And let's just say that, if you didn't come today, I would have been all right tonight because I've learned my way around in darkness."

The blessing, after he left, was now I had light. The unfortunate thing was that, later on that night, I still maneuvered throughout the house, and for the next day or two, as if I had no light. The same thing I did before the light was fixed was the same thing I did after the light was fixed. I had learned my way around in darkness. In other words, maneuvering through darkness had become my norm. I had to get to the place that I had to not just turn the light on, but I had to leave it on to remind myself that I had it simply because I had walked in darkness for so long.

There are some folks who have the light, but they don't leave it on and remind themselves that they have it. If the light was left on, there could never be easy access to darkness. Some folks turn the light on when they need it and turn it off when it's convenient. It behooves us to always desire the light of the Lord, not just when it's convenient.

The text says: You were sometimes darkness but now you are light in the Lord: walk as children of light. When we walk as children of light, darkness will come, but we have light in the Lord. When we walk as children of light, our decisions are God-centered, not situation-centered. When we walk as children of light, God gets the glory, not you. When we walk as children of light, what God says about a matter is more important than what man says about the matter. When we walk as children of light, we can be in the midst of darkness, but we will always stand out. When we walk as children of light, darkness cannot overtake you. When we walk as children of light, we begin to take on the stand that God takes. When we walk as children of light, we will understand that no weapon formed against us will prosper. When we walk as children of light, we'll discern that there are some folks that can mimic light really well but are steeped in darkness. When we walk as children of light, everything that is misaligned can be commanded to come into divine alignment. When we walk as children of light, His Word becomes a lamp unto our feet and a light unto our path.

Jesus turned the light on when he died on Calvary's cross to redeem us from darkness. Jesus turned the light on when they hung him high and stretched him wide. Jesus turned the light on when he shed His blood in exchange for our sins. This day, and every day hereafter, may you keep the light on.

Dear Father, thank you for dying on the cross for us so that those things that we have become accustomed to in the dark will now have your light shone upon them. In Jesus' name, Amen.

DAY 22

TIMING IS EVERYTHING

Ecclesiastes 3:1-8 (KJV): *To everything there is a season, and a time to every purpose under the heaven: ²A time to be born, and a time to die; a time to plant, and a time to pluck up that which is planted; ³A time to kill, and a time to heal; a time to break down, and a time to build up; ⁴A time to weep, and a time to laugh; a time to mourn, and a time to dance; ⁵A time to cast away stones, and a time to gather stones together; a time to embrace, and a time to refrain from embracing; ⁶A time to get, and a time to lose; a time to keep, and a time to cast away; ⁷A time to rend, and a time to sew; a time to keep silence, and a time to speak; ⁸A time to love, and a time to hate; a time of war, and a time of peace.*

One thing about time, unlike anything else, is that it can never be replaced or extended. The only thing you can do with time is use it. Oftentimes, once we realize how much time has passed, we find ourselves asking the question: Where did the time go?

Malcolm X said, "In all our deeds, the proper value and respect for time determines success or failure." Martin Luther King Jr. said, "The time is always right to do what is right." Perhaps you have never heard these quotes from these two African-American leaders, but you may have heard phrases such as "Time waits for no man," "Time is money," "Killing time," "The time is now," "There's no time like the present," "Take time to smell the roses," "Third time's the charm," "Time heals all wounds," "Time's up," "Keeping time," "Making time," "Spending time," and even, "Doing time."

The text shows us there's a time for everything; therefore; if time is everything and in everything, why do we live so carelessly? Life is a totality of the fulfillment of time moments.

No one is ever concerned about that which is inevitably lost as a result of living outside of God's timing and, most importantly, outside of God's will. Everything that happens in God happens in God's timing. We must desire to be in God's timing. In God's timing, what one deems as ordinary events are purposeful events that procreate an end result without you knowing that you are a part of the timing of a God event.

When I was growing up in New York, I played a lot of outside games. I loved playing paddle ball and tennis almost every day. What I didn't do, but always admired was, double Dutch, which is a game in which two long jump ropes turning in opposite directions are jumped by one or more players simultaneously. While watching it in action, I began to understand that successfully jumping the rope was all about timing. Many times, things seen in the natural can help us in the spiritual. I learned a lot of lessons because of double Dutch. One, in particular, was, before you even jump in the rope, you have to hear it, see it, and then jump in. Hear it. See it. And then jump in. Double Dutch requires, at least, three people — one jumping and two turning the rope. In order to make this happen smoothly, the turners have to be in agreement with the one that is jumping. There has to be a balance of rhythm. Sometimes, you see the turners swaying back and forth rhythmically while turning. This enables them to synchronize their timing. But when a turner is not in sync with the jumper and the jumper begins to hear the wrong sound, they will watch the rope for a moment and then insistently say, "Somebody's double handed. I can hear it." Timing is everything! In order to rectify this problem, the jumper stands behind the one that isn't turning right, and hand over hand, she begins to help her turn, until she hears what she needs to hear and sees what she needs to see. Then, she lets her hands go and jumps in. Timing is everything!

As a body of believers, likewise, we need to stand behind the people that need a little help with their timing. We ought to take a lesson or two from double Dutch jumpers. When we don't hear what God says, then we need to begin to help our brothers and sisters with their confessions. When they don't see what God sees, we need to stand behind them and remind them whose they are. We need to tell them, "You are fearfully and wonderfully made. You are more than a conqueror. You are the head and not the tail. You are the elect of God."

We need to stand behind people until we can hear and see what God says about them and their situation. The scripture says: If two of you shall agree on earth as touching anything that they shall ask, it shall be done for them of my Father which is in heaven. Once we can hear it, then we see it. Then, we can let go. Timing is everything in the kingdom. God uses each of us for His time events. Whether we're laughing or crying, planting or reaping, mourning or dancing, God uses us for His time events. Are you available to be used by the Almighty?

Dear Father, even when we don't understand your timing, help us to hear it, see it, and then let go and let God. Thank you. Amen.

DAY 23

CUT OFF THE DEAD STUFF

John 15:1-4 (KJV): *I am the true vine, and my Father is the husbandman.* ² *Every branch in me that beareth not fruit he taketh away: and every branch that beareth fruit, he purgeth it, that it may bring forth more fruit.* ³ *Now ye are clean through the word which I have spoken unto you.* ⁴ *Abide in me, and I in you. As the branch cannot bear fruit of itself, except it abide in the vine; no more can ye, except ye abide in me.*

There comes a time in our lives when we can visibly see God pruning some things and some people out of our lives. The Greek word for pruning (kládema) means cleans. The process isn't always pleasant, but it is needed for growth. In order to prune or cut off some dead stuff, you first have to be familiar with what life looks like; otherwise, you'll cut off the wrong thing at the wrong time.

I enjoy working outside in the yard. The part that I thought I enjoyed most was planting and creating beautiful works of art with flowers in large planters and even in flower beds. Then, I found out that there was something that I enjoyed even more, and that was using a lopper (a large gardening tool with a long handle used for clipping branches) and cutting away old branches. I later found out that the lopper is only useful when it's used correctly. Somehow, I'd spent the first hour or so using this tool the wrong way. I had inverted the tool and was cutting with the dull part, thereby, working against myself. There will be times in your life that you are intentional about cutting away some dead stuff, but that which you

115

are using is working more against you than for you. That's a good place to seek God's pruning power.

Like this text, it was time for me to cut off the branches that were dead, so I began diligently cutting. I cut off all the dead branches that were hanging low but had, somehow, managed to fill up the tree so much that it made the tree look full of life from the street level. It wasn't until I got down inside the tree low enough to see how many dead branches really existed. In other words, I had to view it from the owner's perspective. There are always two perspectives — the street perspective and the owner's perspective. The owner can see stuff that everyone else can't see because they don't have the benefit of being close up and on the property. From the street level, this tree was not only the tallest, but it was also the fullest. There are some things that look really good from afar; in other words, it looks great from the street perspective. Only the creator, only the owner, knows what it looks like down on the inside and close up.

As I was cutting, I noticed that the dead stuff had prevented me from seeing clearly through to the other side of the yard. There are some things in our lives that we won't see clearly unless and until we cut away the dead stuff. While I was cutting away some dead branches, I noticed a vine of poison ivy, but I'd almost missed it because it blended in so well with the tree. It wasn't until I got up underneath as I was cutting away the low, dead branches that I realized that this ivy had wrapped itself around the lowest point or the base of the tree. My neighbor noticed that I was cutting away poison ivy, and he said, "It's a good thing you're cutting that off because it would have eventually choked the life out of the tree and caused it to die."

What am I saying? You've got to get to the place where you realize that there are those people and things in your life that are blending in like everybody else, just to get close enough to you to choke the life out of you, but they're doing it when you're at your lowest point.

In this season, it is imperative to discern who or what is trying to attach themselves to you, mimicking life. Ask God to reveal to you who or what needs to be cut off. Your life depends on it. God has great things in store for you. The true vine desires that we bear much fruit. I invite you to abide in Him today.

Dear Father, there are those people and things in our lives that we need to cut off, and you've made it clear that they are not adding life to us. Thank you in advance for showing us where the dead stuff is, from the Creator's point of view. Amen.

DAY 24

Do What You Heard

James 1:22 (KJV): *But be ye doers of the word, and not hearers only, deceiving your own selves.*

As a child, this phrase was very common in my household. It was always easier to pretend not to hear a thing and not have to do it than to hear it and have to do what I knew I'd heard my mom say:

"Clean up that room!"

"Wash those dishes!"

"What are you doing in there?"

"Hurry up. We've gotta go!"

"Did you wash your hands?"

"Did you study for that test?"

All were very simple questions or commands, but when I was doing what I wanted to do, hearing what my mom wanted me to do required something more of me. When I eventually responded to my mom, it was always "huh" or "what did you say?" To which she would always respond, "Do what you heard."

My parents seldom repeated themselves because, most of the time, I'd heard them the first time, and they knew it. Aren't we, as believers, the same way? Acting as if we don't know what we heard God say? Most of the time, we heard God the first time.

Helen Keller, a well-known American author, political activist, and lecturer, was both blind and deaf. She has been quoted as saying, "After a lifetime in silence and darkness that to be deaf is a greater affliction than to be blind. Hearing is the soul of knowledge and information of a high order. To be cut off from hearing is to be isolated indeed." Hearing is one of the most necessary senses that we can possibly have as human beings. Unfortunately, when one has a hearing loss, they are cut off. Keller goes on to say, "Blindness separates people from things; deafness separates people from people." Hearing loss is an invisible condition. We cannot see hearing loss, only its effects. Because the presence of a hearing loss is not visible, these effects may be attributed to aloofness, confusion, or personality changes. It can only be assumed that, when one doesn't do what they heard, it's because they didn't hear it. Could it be that we have seen the effects of "hearing loss" in the body of Christ? Confusion? Aloofness? Personality changes? Perhaps! We gather on Sundays but immediately forget and can't apply what we heard on Monday! Is it deafness or selective "hearing loss"? I wonder.

Before the writer talks about being a hearer, he opens the chapter from the perspective of the character of man. From the very beginning, he is talking about a tried faith. He tells us that we ought to count it all joy when you fall into divers (various) temptations. What is a "tried faith"? For some of us, within the last thirty days, our faith has been tried. For others, it has happened within the last thirty minutes! Has your faith been on the auction block lately?

A tried faith is when you know what the word of God says about a thing and then circumstances of life come. In other words, Monday came. Your tried faith causes you to put what you heard into action. Your faith becomes tried when what you do does not come into alignment with what you heard and when what you've heard doesn't seem to be applying to you! Your faith is being tried!

When your faith is tried, the real you comes out! Your real character comes out! James is speaking to that person. He speaks about faith and not wavering. He speaks about double mindedness and temptation, being drawn away and lust. And then it says: But be ye doers. That just means you should be a doer. There's something about being a doer that weeds out the masses of people in any line of work, in any family, or in any ministry. There are always going to be those that will talk about it and then those that will be about it.

The chapter begins: Count it all joy when you fall into diverse temptations knowing this that the trying of your faith worketh patience. There is something in me that, when I am drawn away, when I am tempted, stirs up an impatience that doesn't allow God to do what He has to do in me. Patience has to be perfected, and perfection is only complete when that which is in me can be worked out! Being a hearer and not a doer yields to self-deception! You walk around removing yourself from what you heard, thinking that it doesn't apply to you. The Word of God will always apply to you, if not now, it has or it will. In this same chapter and following verse, it says, being a hearer and not a doer is likened to a person looking at himself in the mirror, walking away and forgetting what he looks like. Do what you heard! If the Word of God says, "love your neighbor," then love your neighbor. If the Word of God says, "don't waiver," then don't waiver! If the Word of God says, "don't commit adultery," then don't commit adultery. Do what you heard! When we do what we heard, God is glorified. God's word will never return void, but it will always accomplish that which we send it to do.

Jesus, our Savior and Redeemer, came, bled, suffered, and died because He did what He heard from the Father so that we could have eternal life. I challenge you today to do what you heard the first time. Your life will be the better for it.

Dear Father, there are many things that vie for our attention, causing us to not be tuned in to your voice. Help us to be obedient once we have heard your voice, and then do what we heard. Thank you for always speaking. In Jesus' name, Amen.

DAY 25

HE ROSE, SO I RISE

Luke 24:1-8 (KJV): *Now upon the first day of the week, very early in the morning, they came unto the sepulchre, bringing the spices which they had prepared, and certain others with them.² And they found the stone rolled away from the sepulchre.³ And they entered in, and found not the body of the Lord Jesus.⁴ And it came to pass, as they were much perplexed thereabout, behold, two men stood by them in shining garments:⁵ And as they were afraid, and bowed down their faces to the earth, they said unto them, Why seek ye the living among the dead? ⁶ He is not here, but is risen: remember how he spake unto you when he was yet in Galilee,⁷ Saying, The Son of man must be delivered into the hands of sinful men, and be crucified, and the third day rise again.⁸ And they remembered his words.*

The Resurrection of the Christ cannot be fully discovered or appreciated lest we revisit Friday, the day of desolation and death. It had been a long time coming. Betrayal had run its course. Enmity showed its inevitable consequences on Calvary. Even the faithful followers could only stand at a distance and watch in despair. It is in those loudly spoken last words of the Christ that we hear something more than misery: Father, into thy hands I commit my spirit. In life, if we have been right or wrong, it is, at last, out of our hands and in God's. There are some things in our lives that, when faced with the inevitable, nine times out of ten, we knew it previously. We've either discussed it, recognized it, forgotten it, or dismissed it, but we knew it. When the time finally came for us to deal with this matter, it was too late. I pondered this text because it is important for us to acknowledge the fact that over 2,000 years ago, Jesus the Christ was resurrected on the third day. He defeated death. No matter where you start reading within the synoptic gospels (Matthew, Mark and Luke,), you are eventually going to end up with the finality of Jesus's journey — the Resurrection. Our relationship with the Christ has been and is based on the fact that he bled, suffered, and died for the remission of our sins, so, it appears that this celebratory yet solemn event in the history of Christianity is often relegated to one Sunday in the year and associated with new outfits, Easter bunnies, and colored eggs.

Somehow, the believer has not connected the resurrection power to their own lives. The same authority that Jesus beheld when he was raised from the dead is the same power and authority we have now as children of the most high God! The power in resurrection is the power we have on Monday morning. God has given you authority to release his Word into the atmosphere and change things in your own life. Change your attitude. Change your thinking.

Unfortunately, what has happened in the body of Christ is we have compartmentalized power to only be on Resurrection Sunday. The enemy has hoodwinked and bamboozled the saints of God to become comfortable in celebrating Resurrection Sunday, as long as you don't bring that Resurrection power into Monday. At some point, we must remember His words!

The text says: *And as they were afraid and bowed down their faces to the earth, they said unto them, why seek ye the living among the dead? He is not here but is risen: remember how he spake unto you when he was yet in Galilee, saying, the Son of man must be delivered into the hands of sinful men, and be crucified, and the third day rise again. And they remembered his words.*

Had they remembered, perhaps, they wouldn't have prepared and brought spices to the tomb. Had they remembered they wouldn't have questioned who would roll away the stone. Something happens to the believer when faced with the reality that there will be some things that must come to an end for the glory of God. As a result, the message of the cross is not death and suffering but the power that comes when one dies and is able to live victoriously again in Christ Jesus. The text says: And they remembered. As we worship and remember upon each resurrection day, we must ascertain that the resurrection is the foundation by which we ourselves must live our lives. Your Bible is a record of the promises of God to the believer. The problem is we leave the words in the book and live our lives in an anxious and haphazard manner, as if promises were not given to us. We must be the victors that he died for. We must walk in the authority that was given to us. And they remembered. Your victorious life is not based upon what you can attain but your response to what you remember.

When you remember, you can tell it! When you remember, you can live it! He rose so that the scriptures would be fulfilled! He rose so that we would have eternal life with and in Christ Jesus! He rose so that we would be redeemed by His blood! He rose so that we could be a part of a royal priesthood! He rose so that we could be crucified with Him! He rose so that we would be complete in Him! He rose, so I rise to live as a victor and not a victim! He rose, so I rise to be healed by His stripes! He rose, so I rise to be transformed by the renewing of my mind! If we could just remember His words, we could speak to every disease in our bodies and declare and decree that we are healed of every infirmity! If we could just remember His words, we could live in the liberty wherewith we were called! He rose, so rise to live and be the victorious children of God that we are!

Dear Father, thank you for your resurrection power that goes beyond Resurrection Sunday mornings and enables us to rise as you have risen in our lives. Amen.

MOM'S MEMOS

PRAYER FOR JUDGMENT

Recently, I was stopped by a policeman for exceeding the speed limit. After being given the ticket and seeing my options, I decided to go to court. I had been instructed to ask for a "Prayer for Judgment" by a friend who was a lawyer, and it was only my first violation. Upon going to court, prepared for whatever, I asked if I could ask for prayer for judgment. I was instructed that it would not be necessary to ask. My next step was to appear before the judge. He asked me if I'd had any violations in the past three years. My answer was no. Then, I was asked if I had made any claims to my insurance in the past three years. My answer was no. Immediately, the judge said, "Pay the court ten dollars," and that nothing on my record or license would be affected.

Every day, God shows us his grace in, sometimes, very unique ways. Yes, we reap what we sow, but the reaping is, sometimes, a lesson to be learned and a ten-dollar court fee.

DAY 26

Tracy La'Nai Clark

I'VE GOT POWER

1 Corinthians 4:20 (KJV): *For the kingdom of God is not in word, but in power.*

The word of God renews, comforts, strengthens, and establishes us. These things cannot be done by the persuasive language of men, but by the power of God. What's happening in the church today is that men and women of God are powerless because they have become dependent upon the persuasive language of others as opposed to the demonstration of the spirits power in operation within themselves. God is seeking a people after His own heart, a people that can speak His word in season and out of season, as well as a people that will be able to demonstrate the true power of God. For it is in the demonstration that lives are healed, delivered, and set free, simply because the power of God is at work.

Recently, while vacationing, I had taken several pictures and videos of all the various sights and sounds. In all my excitement, I hadn't noticed that my battery life on my phone had diminished immensely. I realized I had better hurry up and find some power somewhere. I was desperate because my phone was about to shut down completely. What I didn't know was that the theme park that I was in at the time did not openly allow the general public to access their power outlets. There was power, however, just not in visible places. This one device was my only communication back home and my only ability to capture moments as I vacationed. I needed the power immediately. What was a beautiful vacation day, in a

130

moment's time, became catastrophic because I had no power. I, immediately, went on a quest to find a power source. I likened this quest to some in the body of Christ. At any other time in one's life, there is no need to find a power source, as long as you have a full battery. But as soon as things go in the red, you find yourself on a quest to find a power source, and you become desperate. I became desperate in my search for a power source more than I was enjoying the moment of a beautiful vacation day. There I was, walking around the Magic Kingdom, looking down while everything else was happening around me because I was in search of power. The day was slowly going by me, and I had yet to find a source of power. There are some of us that are doing the same thing, looking down out of desperation, instead of looking up. The Bible says: I will look to the hills from whence cometh my help.

We must understand that power can be found where you least expect it. It wasn't until walking out of the restroom that I noticed a power source. Never underestimate where power is. In this past year, many of you may have missed God because of where you thought the power was not. God moves where He chooses. Some folks may attend worship services in a traditional setting with pews and stained-glass windows, while others may break bread and share the Good News at a coffee shop. Don't under estimate where the power of God is.

So, there I was, charging my phone at the exit door of the ladies' restroom. I realized my surroundings were not ideal, but I needed a power source. The stench of where I was, was almost unbearable, but I needed a power source. The need for power kept me there. I was in a desperate situation. That's why we can never say what we won't do. Desperate people do desperate things. In this season, there might be the stench of many things around you. The situation that you're in may not be ideal, but if the power is there, you might need to just bear the stench and get what you came for. Perhaps your being there can change the atmosphere.

As I was standing at the exit of the facilities, in the midst of unfamiliar faces, in the midst of germs, while charging up my cell phone, a young woman who worked as the bathroom attendant looked at me and said, "You can easily go right next door in the comforts of an air-conditioned building and charge up your phone, and you can sit down. They'll even bring you something cool to drink while you wait."

Just for a second, I wondered, why is this woman, who doesn't know me, giving me information, that I didn't inquire of her? Don't we do that? In this season of your life, not only should we not underestimate where power is, but we also shouldn't underestimate who knows how to access power. When God sends someone your way, despite where you might find them, they very well might have the solution to your problems. God uses people, and those people may not always be in the ideal places that you desire, but they know how to access power.

Our text says: The kingdom of God is not just talking, but it is living by God's power. In this new season of our lives, we ought to live by the demonstration of the power of God. I declare and decree, "We have power!" Power to tread on scorpions, not be afraid of them! We have power. Power to speak those things that be not as though they are! We have power, power to be equipped and not whipped by the circumstances of life. We have power,

power to be the light in a dark world. We have power, power to know that God is our refuge and strength, a very present help in time of trouble. We have power!

God has given us dominion and power over the enemy, and nothing shall, by any means, hurt us! In this new season, we have power to excel in all things, at all times, with all people, under every circumstance. In this new year, let us celebrate creativity and the diversity of all humanity. In this new year, we walk in divine power to be fruitful. God desires greatness from our lives, and we shall receive power from on high and walk therein, that we might be change agents for those who God sends our way. Why not receive His power today?

Dear Father, thank you for giving us power, that we might be effectual disciples in your kingdom, leading others to you, not in word but through demonstration. Amen.

DAY 27

FINISH WHAT
YOU STARTED

2nd Corinthians 8:10-11 (The Message Bible): *So here's what I think: The best thing you can do right now is to finish what you started last year and not let those good intentions grow stale.*

A new year, often, brings the start of new things. New diets. New attitudes. New ways of thinking. New endeavors. New relationships. New vehicles. And new ideas. But the truth of the matter is, there's nothing wrong with finishing what you started last year. Many people have no problem starting something new (i.e. school, diets, or relationships), but something happens midstream, around February or March, and they are not able to follow through with what they started. Therefore, instead of starting something new, why not finish what you started last year?

There are many endeavors that you started in the previous year that you didn't finish. You started it! It took up your time. It sounded good. You worked on it for a little while. You had to do something, so you started! Your intentions were good last year. You started something, but it wasn't effective, so you worked it, perhaps, because ego got in the way, but it wasn't effective. Oftentimes, we just need to go back and look at our motives. Look at our intentions. Perhaps, do some introspective thinking. Ask yourself, what was going on at the time that made me start something? Why didn't I complete it?

When we let God in to do God's work, we can be confident in knowing that we are on the right track. God has great things planned for his people, but sometimes, it requires waiting, and waiting requires discipline. At some point in our lives, anything worth having requires waiting. And if we must wait, why not just wait on the Lord? The problem is we don't like to wait.

We microwave our food. We eat out rather than wait for something to thaw out and then prepare it. We flip channels quickly when a commercial comes on because we don't want to wait. We change lanes rather than wait behind a car that's moving slower than us. We leave items in the store rather than wait in a long line. At some point in time, we have to wait. The Bible says: They that wait on the Lord shall renew their strength. Waiting will result in increased strength. When you don't wait on God, you exhaust your own strength.

In this next season, finish what you started. Don't be moved by the next big thing that calls your attention; instead, focus on the thing that God put in you to do, the thing that only you can do. That's the thing that we are called to accomplish. What a tragedy it would be to leave this world having never completed anything, just a lot of false starts. God has great things in store for you, but only you can finish what you started.

Dear Father, when we are tempted to begin a new thing at the onset of a new year, remind us of the work that you ordained, the work that you have placed in us to complete. Thank you. In Jesus' name, Amen.

DAY 28

HE STILL SPEAKS

John 14:26 (KJV): *But the Helper, the Holy Spirit, whom the Father will send in my name, he will teach you all things and bring to your remembrance all that I have said to you.*

While walking along a beautiful trail in the park, I came across the end of the walkway, which had bumps in the concrete before stepping down into the street. I wasn't quite sure of its purpose, so I inquired once I returned home and found out that those blister-like bumps, also known as "truncated domes and detectible warning pavers," were a part of "tactile paving" (meaning, paving that can be felt). I found out that it helps the visually impaired detect when they are about to leave the sidewalk and enter the street. In other words, it lets them know that a change is about to take place.

After learning about this, I thought, the Holy Spirit provides the believer with these same benefits. Before we step out into unsafe territory, before we make moves that could ultimately harm us, before we make decisions that could be to our detriment, the Holy Spirit gives us a warning within our own spirit to let us know that a change in pattern is about to take place. We have time to make the right decision if we would just listen. Have you paid attention to the Holy Spirit in your daily walk? Perhaps, give the Holy Spirit a try. He still speaks.

Dear Father, thank you for sending the Holy Spirit to be our helper and guide along our life's journey. Enable us to listen to the Spirit's voice and follow when He speaks. Amen.

DAY 29

LOOK STRAIGHT AHEAD AND KEEP MOVING FORWARD

Hebrews 11:1 (KJV): *Now faith is the substance of things hoped for, the evidence of things not seen.*

The Body of Christ has become very familiar with the language of faith. We know what it is supposed to sound like. We know what it looks like, but seldom can we demonstrate it in and through our lives. Martin Luther King Jr said, "Faith is taking the first step, even when you don't see the whole staircase." Billy Graham said, "The greatest legacy one can pass on to one's children and grandchildren is not money or other material things accumulated in one's life, but rather a legacy of character and faith."

Faith is imperative to every aspect of our daily life. Faith is strengthened because of one's relationship with God. There are times that our faith is stretched and pulled upon through life's adversities. We often speak the words of faith when life sends us a moment of victory. We immediately speak defeat when life has sent us trials. Faith is necessary to persevere. There are times when we may find ourselves getting discouraged in the process of persevering. God wants us to persevere. When these times occur, we need to persevere because there is a great work that needs to be accomplished in us and through us. The text says: Now faith is the substance of things hoped for, the evidence of things not seen. It is not faith when we're persevering after what we can see! The reason why many people have so little faith is because they are responding to a now faith was instead of now faith is! A faith was is something you've already seen! You can identify it! You can recall it! You can shout about it! You can sing about it! You can even stand up and testify about it. You know what it looks like. You know what it sounds like. Now you're all excited because you're rejoicing in a now faith was moment! But a now faith is, is a pressing faith! The kind of faith that has seen absolutely nothing. The kind of faith that steps out of boats. The kind of faith that goes around touching hems of garments. The kind of faith that sits by the sides of the pool believing that, eventually, somebody will put you in! The kind of faith that believes those bones can live. The kind of faith that, when tossed in life's fiery furnace, still causes you to say, "The God we serve is able!" The kind of faith that says, "I don't have a rainy-day fund, but I trust God." Rent might be late this month, but I trust God. I trust God in my now! A now faith says, "Move forward anyhow." A now faith moves when it doesn't look like it's working. When things aren't quite coming together, move forward anyhow! It doesn't take faith to stand in one spot and do nothing. Trust God and move forward. A now faith speaks always in the present. I am healed! I am delivered! I am forgiven! I am blessed! I am prosperous! I am favored! I'm talking about a now faith.

When I taught students with different abilities, I not only loved my students, but I would go the extra mile to make sure they were understood. Some time ago, there were some teachers that shared with me that my students never spoke to them when they were in the hallway. They said they looked forward and never responded to them. They emphatically suggested that I should say something to them about their behavior. I responded as a parent would, defending their own child, "The reason why they don't speak to you while walking in the hallway is because you have nothing to do with where they're going!"

What am I saying? Faith looks ahead and keeps moving forward, knowing that there is an appointed destiny. As you travel this journey, you cannot allow things and people to interfere with where you're going. It's imperative to focus on God. It is imperative to look ahead and focus on the things that God has for your hands to do. Distractions in this season will take your eyes off Him. Unless they are assigned to get you to your destination, you don't need the dead weight. You don't need the distraction. You still must get to your set place!

Scripture says in Luke 9:51: And it came to pass, when the time was come that he should be received up, he steadfastly set his face to go to Jerusalem. If Jesus himself had to keep focused, steadfastly setting His face to his destined place, because of the assignment that was on His life, how much more should we, those that are seeking to be with Him when he returns, set ours? Keep looking ahead and move forward. God has a mighty plan for your life. Don't let anything distract you now.

Dear Father, when the distractions of life come our way, help us to keep our eyes upon you, stay in faith and move forward. Amen.

DAY 30

TOMORROW COULD BE A SNOW DAY

John 10:10 (KJV): The thief cometh not but for to steal, kill and destroy, but I've come that you might have life and have it to the full (more abundantly).

Life has a way of changing in an instant. What made you think you were going to see today? When you woke up this morning, did you automatically know that you were going to have vision? Speech? The ability to walk? The amazing thing about life is, we never know what the next moment will hold. Our lives can change in an instant. It is in that place of oblivion and vulnerability that we are humbled and reminded daily that we can do nothing without God; our sole dependence is upon Him. Because tomorrow is not promised, why do so many live their lives like robots? Wake up, take the kids to the sitters, clock in, have lunch, clock out, go home and do it all over again the next day. They never really experience life or enjoy their families and friends and seeing places they've never seen.

Life is meant to be enjoyed, appreciated, and loved. God created each of us to be in relationship with one other, but so often, we busy ourselves and hide behind our jobs, our positions, our homes, our responsibilities, or our things-to-do lists and never really enjoy life. So, what you took a sick day and you weren't sick? Sometimes, you may just need to do what you enjoy. Decompress, plant flowers, play music, dance as if no one was looking, paint, cook, color in a coloring book, binge on movies, and the list could go on. Whatever makes you happy. Why not live your life as if tomorrow were a snow day?

When I was a teacher, I would get so excited as I watched the snow vigorously fall at night, knowing, without a shadow of a doubt, that school would be closed the next day. I would plan what I was going to watch on TV, plan out my favorite breakfast, and commence sitting in front of the television, waiting for my school's name to scroll across the bottom of the screen. Such a welcoming five words: School will be closed tomorrow. I reveled in the idea of how exciting the day was going to be, piddling around the house, working on a few projects here and there, watching my favorite movies, reading a good book, just enjoying the day of endless possibilities.

Life should be just like that! It is meant to be enjoyed. You become very creative on a snow day. You read. You watch TV. You play games with the kids. You bake. You talk on the phone to people you haven't spoken to in months. You enjoy social media. The creativity that comes with a snow day is amazing! We are creative beings, made in the image of the Master Creator!

Do something different today because tomorrow is not promised. Make more memories, not more bills. Respond to life differently. Act as if tomorrow could be a snow day. Plan to enjoy it because life is too short. When it's all said and done, would you much rather your legacy have been he/she was such a hard worker, or he/she really enjoyed life and enjoyed it abundantly? God knows the plans He has for our life. Plans to prosper us and not harm us. Plans to give us a hope and a future. Your future looks bright! Why not enjoy it as if tomorrow were a snow day?

Dear Father, help us to enjoy life as you have ordained. Show us how to live an abundant life, not concerning ourselves with what we cannot control but enjoying every moment that you have given unto us. Amen.

MOM'S MEMOS

NOT IN USE

Recently, I saw sign on a bathroom door that read "Out of order. Not in use." I thought, This should be put on many professing Christians. We are not about the business of our Father. We have not taken the great commission seriously. Christ said, "Go." We simply go to church, which is great; however, that is a small portion of our tasks.

Too many of us are not in use and are out of order. Perhaps, we need to hear the gospel preached more to remind us of our use.

PRAYER OF SALVATION

Jesus Christ, the Son of the living God, bled, suffered, and died for our sins that we might have eternal life with Him. However, the only way we can be with Him when He returns, is if we confess our sins and ask Him into our hearts. The scripture says, in Romans 10:9-10, 13: *That if thou shalt confess with thy mouth the Lord Jesus, and shalt believe in thine heart that God hath raised him from the dead, thou shalt be saved. For with the heart man believeth unto righteousness; and with the mouth confession is made unto salvation. For whoever shall call upon the name of the Lord shall be saved.*

Would you like to confess Jesus Christ as your Lord and Savior today? Say this simple prayer.

Lord Jesus, I repent of my sins. Come into my heart. I make you my Lord and Savior. Amen.

If you prayed this prayer with me, the angels are rejoicing over another soul that has given his or her life to Christ. You've made the best decision of your life. Stay in faith. Connect with an assembly of believers that teach and preach the Good News of Jesus Christ. Stay in communion with God. Things won't always be easy, but never forget God is in control. When life presents you questions that seem out of reach, God has provided the answers, in the Word of God. God bless you and your new walk in Christ.

CPSIA information can be obtained
at www.ICGtesting.com
Printed in the USA
BVHW041920250619
551941BV00016B/124/P